Alan Grant

Against the Clock

**Work study and
incentive schemes**

Pluto Press

Alan Grant worked in the printing
industry for twenty years and is still a
member of NATSOPA (now SOGAT 82).
During that time he was a Father of the
Chapel for thirteen years and a plant
convenor for seven years, and has
negotiated on and worked under work
study and incentive conditions. He
currently works full-time in trade-union
education.

First published in 1983 by
Pluto Press Limited,
The Works, 105a Torriano Avenue,
London NW5 2RX

Cover designed by Colin Bailey

Set by Wayside Graphics, Clevedon,
Avon BS21 7JG
Printed in Great Britain by
Photobooks Limited, Barton Manor,
St Philips, Bristol BS2 0RN
Bound by W. H. Ware, Tweed Road,
Clevedon, Avon BS21 6QG

British Library Cataloguing in Publication Data
Grant, Alan
    Against the clock – (workers' handbooks)
    1. Job analysis
    I. Title   II. Series
    658.4′032   HF 5549.5.J6

ISBN 0-86104-369-3

Contents

List of tables and diagrams

Acknowledgements

Thanks to Pat Kinnersly, Jim Sutherland (Solihull Trade Union Studies Centre) and John Fisher (West Midlands WEA), for reading the manuscript and making some very helpful suggestions; to Sheila for boosting my confidence and making the space for me to write; and to comrades in the trade-union movement for their shared wisdoms and experiences.

To the memory of 'Dai'
who didn't like work study much either.

Introduction

> **These fifty redundancies are what we call a tree-pruning exercise; the only trouble is that this is the tenth I've attended in the last year and we haven't saved a bloody tree yet.**
>
> **Full-time officer, 1970**

To many trade unionists, work study means little more than 'time and motion' and the stopwatch. Typical reactions reflect a preoccupation with work study as a means of rate-fixing and a general resentment at being watched and recorded. Although conventional work study involves all these things they are only the tip of the iceberg. For trade unionists involved in negotiating on working conditions and jobs, it is essential to see work study as something much wider than a system for setting up a bonus scheme.

There are countless reasons why work should be studied; to make the working environment healthier and safer, to eliminate soul-destroying jobs, to make work more interesting and fulfilling. Work study is not aimed in any of these directions; in fact it is more likely to worsen these aspects of our working lives than to improve them. This is because work study is an employer's tool to be used *by* management *for* management objectives. It can never be completely neutral.

At the heart of all management objectives lie **control** and **reduction of costs** and when management pursues these objectives, the consequences for workers inevitably extend beyond the size of the wage packet. They affect the way we work, the number of us who work, our health, trade-union organisation and the right to have a say in the day-to-day decisions made at the workplace. Does it make sense to talk about 'management control' when it is quite apparent to most people that employers and managements already have control over the enterprises which they own and manage? They may not get their own way all the time but it is entirely their decision whether or not a firm opens or closes. The more obvious limitations on managerial control are usually identified as the borderlines between arbitrary decision-making by management and collective bargaining between management and unions, usually over pay, jobs, hours and, lately, health, safety and pensions.

But this is still only part of the picture; ordinary workers, and especially skilled workers, often exercise daily control over the way they work. Many jobs require workers to use their experience and knowledge in making judgements, solving problems and using initiative. Where workers use these mental faculties to any significant degree, then it is *they* who are momentarily exercising control. Management is temporarily at the mercy of those workers. Management control is aimed at removing that power of decision-making from the workers and installing it within management, where its use can be trusted. This process has resulted in jobs which are so narrowly defined that they are fit only for zombies, human robots and, eventually, real robots.

All this is perpetrated in the name of 'efficiency', or 'productivity' and is all about **costs**. Every management strives to reduce costs, particularly the cost of labour which is one of the few items over which it can exert an influence, through collective bargaining. In private industry, every pound saved in costs increases profits in good years and reduces losses in bad years. The **public services**, being continually subjected to budget restrictions (usually called cash limits), are massive users of work study. Public sector unions have been forced to accept these techniques as a way to get bonus schemes and so mitigate the worst effects of low pay. This has seriously reduced job opportunities in the public sector, and severely undermined the quality and quantity of services provided to the community.

Employers and their academic allies in the fields of industrial psychology, industrial sociology and industrial engineering have been applying their minds to ways and means of increasing managerial control for the past eighty years or so. In the constant search for the 'best way', the 'cheapest method' and the 'shortest time', workers are seldom asked what they want from a lifetime of employment. In fact, so powerful has management logic become, that trade unionists are hard pushed to come up with anything beyond decent pay and working conditions, if and when they are asked. Trade-union opposition to the more destructive manifestations of the pursuit of profit has led employers to develop more sophisticated techniques to control organised labour.

A hundred years ago it was enough for employers to rely on simple **coercion** – the sack, wage cuts, piecework systems with no fall-back rate, and criminal law. The newer methods have inquired into workers' **'motivation'**, and the social scientist has produced job evaluation, profit-sharing, job enrichment and bogus participation schemes aimed at promoting the 'community of interest' philosophy of employer/employee relations. However, when the stakes are high enough and the time is judged to be right, it is with consummate ease that modern management reverts to type and destroys any remaining credibility in the myth of 'harmony in industry'. The behaviour of managements at British Leyland from 1979 to 1982 and at *The Times* in 1978 testify to this.

For these reasons, work study cannot be regarded as a mutual solution to a common problem between employers and workers. Most managements know that workers will not normally co-operate willingly in having their every movement scrutinised, unless they can be tempted. This is where the **incentive scheme** comes in, the pot of gold which mysteriously appears to enrich everybody and the price of which will be picked up by the workers at some future date.

Most managements also know that work study and a new incentive scheme will not produce a lasting 'solution'. The continual struggle between the conflicting interests of employers and workers means a continual search for new solutions, often aided and abetted by the government. A piecework system is replaced by an incentive scheme based upon time standards because, allegedly, the old system is 'out of date' or 'inefficient'; later, often depending upon the level of workplace trade-union organisation, the new scheme is replaced by measured day work and a new pay structure. Profit-sharing and value-added schemes will also appear as 'good ideas' at some stage; after these, the employer may well revert to individual or departmental incentives.

The essential point is that an employer faced with trade-union organisation which is democratic, well informed and prepared to act collectively will, as a conscious management strategy, keep **changing the rules**. Before the workforce gets on top of the new system and begins to exert some control over its workings, it will be changed. This can be seen in a number of industries over the past few years.

In coal mining the National Power Loading Agreement of the late sixties replaced a system of pit-based piecework schemes with an industry-wide pay structure aimed at, amongst other things, eliminating wage demands based upon comparability with the best-paid pits. By 1977, the National Coal Board had successfully sold (or re-sold) the idea of pit-based incentives – probably motivated by the solidarity shown by the miners in the national pay disputes of 1972 and 1974. British Leyland, since 1968, has moved from piecework to measured day work to a company-wide wage structure and, currently, to plant-based incentives.

Ringing the changes and producing new ideas are all part of management's struggle to retain or increase its control over the workplace. Employers have always exerted some influence over the time it takes to carry out a particular job, usually with the aid of the crude techniques mentioned earlier. Only in the last 80 years or so have they shown a consuming interest in **methods** of work. This interest was stimulated by the development of so-called **'scientific management'**. Driven by the cannibalistic principles of capitalism, employers inquired into every conceivable avenue of cost-cutting to keep or expand their share of the market at the expense of their competitors. They began to ask two questions about the ways in which work is performed; not just **how long** will the job take but **how** is it done? Answering the second question meant studying the way people worked, understanding traditional skills, learning how workers applied new skills and how they organised their own work.

This was an area of control which had traditionally remained with the workers but which had been gradually eroded with the progress of the industrial revolution. Employers extracted these remaining controls by fragmenting traditional jobs into smaller tasks, a process which went hand-in-hand with the developing technologies of mass production and the assembly line. Employers discovered that the work **method** used determined the **time** it took, and time meant **money**; seconds saved here, minutes there meant dollars and pounds in the long run.

The automobile industry is the classic example. That the application of these techniques in Detroit meant redundancies at Citroen, was hardly a matter to concern the management of General Motors. That the pursuit of job division and sub-division, enabling the application of micro-electronics to motor manufacture, destroyed the employment prospects of thousands of workers, is of no consequence to Toyota.

The result is a concept of efficiency which has no morality; it determines the way we work, the products we make (or do not make), the way health care is provided and, ultimately, the designation of industrial disease and environmental pollution as 'acceptable risks'.

The arrival of micro-electronics in the workplace does not herald the end of developments in management techniques for controlling labour. New technology is an aid to control. Despite the wonders of the Fiat factories, the robot take-over is some way off – human beings are more adaptable and still cheaper in many cases. Work study retains its popularity among British managements as a way of increasing labour productivity and reducing costs. In spite of their notoriously poor investment record in the past fifty years, British companies still attempt to compete with foreign employers who have invested. Many will have to choose between investing massive sums in new methods and cranking up the rate of labour productivity through cheaper means, such as work study and incentives. Many will opt for the cheaper means.

To illustrate this point; a GMWU steward once asked me to cast an eye over a new incentive scheme which management had proposed to the members. My first question was to ask why the company wanted a new scheme in the first place. It seemed that the management was anxious to increase output without taking on more labour. Amongst other things, the company manufactured lead strips for the building industry and, with the technology available, could only produce them in ten-metre lengths. But the customers required continuous coils which meant that the ten-metre lengths had to be soldered together to form a continuous strip. Suspicious that a company supplying materials to the building industry in the middle of its worst depression this century should want to *increase* output, the steward made further inquiries.

It transpired that the company's major competition, in West Germany, had developed a machine which could produce continuous lead strip much more cheaply and was securing a large share of the UK market. The British company's response was to attempt to raise labour productivity as a means of lowering unit costs, in an endeavour to retain some hold on its markets. Rather than invest, it chose the cheaper method and will, no doubt, berate its employees for their laziness and inflexibility whilst making un-favourable comparisons with West German workers in the years ahead.

Workers and their representatives will continue to face pro-posals from managements for work study, incentive schemes and productivity deals; members will continue to seek pay settlements which meet the rising cost of living; and employers will continue to insist that settlements are self-financing. These situations are faced daily in workplaces all over the country and, while it may be pertinent to point out that life in a competitive capitalist society will always be like this, such wisdoms are of little immediate comfort. Until the trade-union and working-class movements gain widespread membership support for genuine alternatives, even the most class-conscious of shop stewards will find themselves, one day, across the table from a management consultant.

This Workers' Handbook aims to provide practical assistance to trade unionists who have to deal with work study and related incentive schemes. Its approach follows the sequence of events which is likely to occur where work study is introduced for the first time. It seeks to explain the technical aspects of work study and to indicate the pitfalls, the negotiating issues, the benefits to manage-ment and some alternatives. This approach should be useful to: workers familiar with work study as a simple form of rate-fixing; those who are already operating under work study agreements; and those who are facing work study and incentive schemes for the first time.

Most chapters contain a summary of the main points as well as a checklist of negotiating issues. I have refrained from including a 'model' work study agreement as such a thing is no more possible than inventing a fool-proof system for winning at roulette.

You will very quickly notice that the book is fundamentally anti-work study; this is because it is based upon years of personal experience of working under work study-based incentives, negoti-ating about work study and dealing with the problems which it raises. This experience has been considerably aided and supported by the views and information communicated by comrades in the trade-union movement. For me, the theories came later.

My own opposition to work study extends beyond the basic antagonism which most trade-union activists have learned to feel towards employers. It cannot be sustained by dislike of individual members of management, by certain management techniques or by the amazing hypocrisy contained in most public utterances by senior managers. Management itself is a tool of the employer and managers as a group can do no more than strive to meet employers' objectives – that is their function and purpose. In a capitalist society, management is locked in conflict, not only with the workers they seek to control, but also with the managements of competing enterprises. The whole structure is based upon conflict and must, therefore, be irrational. There are countless books dedicated to exposing and documenting the flaws inherent in modern capitalism. I do not have to repeat those arguments here but there should be ample evidence in the following pages to suggest that the methods which modern managements employ to control workers are not only anti-trade union but anti-human.

Most workers want nothing more from any political or economic system than a job, security and decent working conditions. The knowledge and experience that work study undermines each one of these fundamental objectives is enough to sustain my own personal opposition. The search for alternatives leads to the inevitable conclusion that the problem lies not with any particular management technique, but with the objectives that drove management to adopt those techniques in the first place.

Part One

Work Study

1.
What is work study?

To many workers, work study is simply a complicated and irritating means to an end, the end being the opportunity to work on some kind of incentive bonus scheme resulting in higher earnings. Quite often these bonus schemes are required to be **'self-financing'**, with the common result that the wages of workers eventually made redundant through the application of work study are spread among those who remain. This is not to say that there is no merit in eliminating the waste of resources such as fuel and materials, or the waste created through incompetent decision-making and inefficient management. However, the word **'waste'** tends to mean different things to different people. Most of us would regard every person on the dole as being wasted, yet employers' solutions to reducing 'waste' in their own organisations often involve lengthening the dole queue.

Savings can be made by using materials more economically, by eliminating the causes of sub-standard work and by minimising delays and breakdowns. To many employers the most expensive resource is **labour** and raising the rate of labour productivity is usually the most attractive method of reducing costs. Few employers can negotiate over the price they pay for materials, electricity, rent and rates, but they do exercise a dominant power over the price they pay for labour. Their influence is exercised in two ways – through controlling the size of the individual's wage packet, and through controlling the total number of workers they actually employ. By manipulating these two methods of control, the employer is able to perpetuate the myth that bonus schemes create a pool of new money which can enrich everybody concerned. In fact, the largest proportion of this mythical pool comes from the wages of workers who were dismissed and not replaced or who were not taken on in the first place.

Work study provides management with a systematic means of examining all the factors which contribute to the organisation's costs. These factors include:

- the actual **product** or service being produced;
- the **materials** used;
- the production **methods** employed;
- the activities and **skills** of the workers involved; and
- the **time** it takes to carry out the work.

Detailed studies are undertaken of existing work methods, layouts and workers' activities and all necessary information is carefully recorded. While workers may see these studies as tiresome procedures to be endured for the future privilege of working to an incentive scheme, employers see them as an opportunity to be seized with both hands. The initial stages of work study produce something which managements often lack – information.

How many trade unionists would willingly submit themselves to detailed scrutiny of the way they work if it were not for the carrot of a bonus being dangled before them? The labour movement can produce thousands of examples of disputes which occurred when an intruder was detected making furtive observations and taking notes. Work study consultants are well aware of their historical reputation as 'shop floor spies' and of the bitter antagonism they have encountered in well-organised shops all over the country; indeed, all over the world. With the growth of strong workplace trade-union organisation, the practitioners have had to change their approach. They now praise the virtues of 'consultation' with unions, of 'joint participation' in the study and of 'agreement' at all stages. Of course, if the local trade-union organisation is weak or non-existent, these apparently democratic niceties will be overlooked.

Work study consultants' apparent concern with their acceptability and image is in reality a simple piece of self-preservation. Whether they are individual practitioners or members of a firm of consultants, their livelihood depends upon the next contract. Any firm of consultants which gains a reputation as a trouble-maker is likely to find itself running out of customers. Some employers may find the consultative procedures somewhat irksome and unnecessary, but the consultants will explain that 'gaining the workers' confidence' and 'getting them involved' are valuable pieces of psychology which will pay dividends in the long run.

Apart from the rare occasions when, in an unguarded moment, a worker produces a clever little idea which could eliminate three or four jobs, employers and consultants are not really interested in the views of trade unionists or the protestations of their representatives. But if 'consultation' can remove obstruction and smooth the path towards its objectives, management will patiently indulge. Those **objectives** are always the same:

■ information about the current state of affairs;

■ information as a reliable basis upon which to make change; and

■ change itself, to increase the employer's control over the organisation.

The process may begin with an examination of the organisation's cost structures and the goods and services produced. The aim will be to sort out where the organisation is spending its money, to locate areas for closer examination and, perhaps, to make fairly broad and tentative proposals for change. As the organisation is scrutinised in greater detail, the techniques of work study which are more familiar to trade unionists will begin to be used. There are two basic features of work which employers will wish to analyse and control: **how** work is done; and **how long** it takes to do it. To provide answers to these questions, work study is separated into two specific operations: these are known as method study and work measurement.

Method study:

a) examine and record existing methods of work, including machinery, equipment, workers' activities and work organisation;
b) devise new methods and layouts using the information from a);
c) simplify and eliminate operations where possible;
d) draw up new methods in writing; and
e) install the new methods and check that they are adhered to.

Work measurement:

f) measure each operation to establish standard times for all operations using the stopwatch or other measurement techniques; and
g) issue standard times as 'target' times for all jobs and operations.

Part One of this book looks at these steps in detail and discusses the problems and issues involved for workers.

2.
Method study

The purpose of method study / method study and control / method study and productivity / activity sampling / tasks and elements / summary / checklist

The purpose of method study

Employers will argue that there is little point in timing a particular job until they can be sure that the method of work used by the operative is the **'best'** method available. The obvious place to start is to make a detailed study of the methods of work in current use. This entails observing and recording the following:
- the way materials and parts move around the workplace;
- the machinery in use and the way in which it is used;
- the way teams of workers work together;
- the way in which an individual worker carries out particular tasks;
- the ways in which instructions and orders are given; and
- the system for booking and checking the quality and quantity of the work done.

In the first two cases, the study engineers will be trying to identify unnecessary movements of materials and parts so as to reduce delays, materials wastage, excessive handling and idle time and generally to streamline the flow of work. At this stage, quite wide-ranging changes may be proposed, such as moving a department from one place to another, combining departments, purchasing new handling equipment or even introducing new technology. How far these changes are taken will depend, to a large degree, on how much money the employer is prepared to invest. This will probably have been extensively discussed before trade unionists are invited to become involved.

Where method studies are carried out in a particular workplace for the first time, a considerable amount of information will probably be recorded. Various charts and diagrams will be drawn up to show material movements, worker movements and machine utilisation. Often this paperwork will be identified by rather technical names such as 'Flow Process Charts', 'Flow Diagrams' and 'Multiple Activity Charts'. Despite the jargon they are not difficult to understand and they will usually be summarised so that the essential information can be quickly digested. Copies of this paperwork should be provided to union representatives.

As a general approach to examining methods of work, consultants and study engineers are trained to take *nothing* for granted. They are aware that in many cases middle and senior management know very little about the details of work organisation, demarcation and job skills. They also know that often a job is done in a particular way for no better reason than that it has always been done that way. So consultants prefer to make their own observations rather than depend upon what they are told by management or by workers, and in making these observations they will be aiming to establish:

■ **what** is actually done;
■ **where** it is done;
■ **when** it is done;
■ **who** does it; and
■ **how** it is done.

These questions may seem fairly obvious and the answers assumed to be common knowledge. However, especially in workplaces where trade-union organisation is strong, method study may present the employers with their first real opportunity to investigate what actually happens, day in day out, on the shop floor or in the office. When that scrutiny is applied to the methods which workers use, how they organise their work and how they actually spend their time, the total knowledge gained by upper management is considerable. Part of the information may expose management inefficiencies in organising materials, parts and workloads; it may also indicate poor maintenance procedures, worn-out machinery and badly-designed work areas. In fact, the studies may simply reinforce many of the complaints that workers and supervisors have been making for years. However, employers tend to attribute greater credibility to the advice for which they pay than to that which comes free.

Ultimately, the activities of workers will be subject to the most intensive study. At one level, a method study will examine the **pace** of work, delays, breaks and rest periods, machine speeds, 'unofficial' practices, shortcuts, ways in which workers help each other, demarcations and restrictions. At another level, workers' **skills** will be studied, recorded and analysed in the form of the sequence of movements and operations involved in carrying out each task.

The aim of method study at this level is to simplify the job, to eliminate movements and operations considered to be unnecessary and, where possible, to eradicate tasks where workers have traditionally chosen for themselves the methods of work to be used.

Method study and control

The recording and examination of current methods of work adds considerable strength to the employer's arm in negotiations with union representatives on workloads, demarcation and job control. So-called restrictive practices and working customs, which may have helped to protect jobs and to make work more pleasant, will be attacked as a source of 'waste' and their removal made a condition of the impending bonus scheme.

It is vital that the membership is aware of the price they may be called upon to pay when they decide whether or not to accept work study. If it is agreed to allow work study it is important to discuss in advance the conditions under which method study may be applied. In practice, a **clear agreement that new work methods can only be introduced with the approval of the membership** should provide breathing space in which to consider the implication of the employer's proposals.

The next issue concerns the study methods to be used. Charts and diagrams are one thing, but your members may strongly resent the use of cine film, for example. An agreement requiring management to submit study techniques for union approval can help to ensure that only **mutually-agreed study methods** are used. (One employer who attempted to use a cine camera against the wishes of a particular group of workers merely succeeded in gaining some excellent footage of idle machinery, bizarre impersonations of John Cleese and a rather large, uncovered backside.)

The aims and objectives of method study can be influenced by trade unionists through **negotiated agreements** and **organised monitoring** of job changes. While employers will want to find faster and cheaper methods of work which, as we have seen, are seldom in the long-term interests of workers, trade unionists can demand that other factors be taken into account. There is no reason why the brief should not be widened to include the elimination of risks to health and safety, improvement of the working environment, removal of 'ghetto' jobs which do not permit workers to socialise, and elimination of excessive physical labour.

All these issues will have to be raised with the membership to promote genuine discussion before any consultants or work study engineers are allowed into the workplace. Union representatives must ensure that the members are fully aware of the potential increase in control which the employer can achieve through method study. Representatives should not assume that they know everything about every job: the members actually doing the jobs to be studied must be fully involved. Only with full membership understanding and support will it be possible to negotiate the kind of agreements mentioned earlier.

Method study and productivity

Method study is essentially an exercise in gathering information, analysing it and making proposals for change. By **analysing** current methods the study engineer is able to experiment with new methods on paper, without disrupting production, until the proposal most acceptable to the employer is drafted, checked and implemented. New methods of work are likely to be fully written out and compared with existing methods so that estimates of productivity increases and cost savings can be made. Method changes are likely to affect who does what, where, when and how, as well as the total number of jobs involved.

Access to these estimates is vital to union negotiators if they are to assess not only the likely impact upon the quality and quantity of jobs but also the gains which the employer expects to make. Method study offers the employer far greater opportunities to extend management control and to increase productivity than work measurement ever will. In the past, trade unionists have often been so obsessed with the issues of work measurement, such as rating and the stopwatch, and with the intricacies of the incentive scheme, that the savings made through method study have all accrued to the employer by default.

Although there are two distinct phases in the application of work study – method study and work measurement, the entire operation is best looked at as three separate stages:

stage one: studying and recording current work methods and activities;

stage two: analysing the information, assessing it and proposing changes; and

stage three: setting work standards for the accepted method of working.

Even if employers only complete stage one, they have gained a tremendous amount of information about the way the workplace functions, and this will be of considerable value in future negotiations. Stage two provides the first opportunity to use that information to good effect by providing a detailed analysis of what is possible within the limits of available finance. Stage three sets up the basic data for budgeting, costing, pricing, work programming, labour programming and so on. The incentive scheme is simply tacked on at the end as a means of ensuring that the workforce adheres to the new standards and targets. All too often, trade-union anxiety about the prospect of incentive working is allowed to obscure the increases in productivity and control which the employer obtains from **each single stage** in the above procedure.

An agreement to accept work study should be accompanied by the condition that management will provide comprehensive information on **current** productivity levels (i.e. *before* work study is applied). This information could consist of statistics on output, working hours, wage costs and other costs. It should be presented in a form which union representatives can understand and not in whatever form suits management. It is a serious mistake to be intimidated into pretending that jargon and figures are understood when, initially, they seem to make no sense at all. Many managers have the same problem which is why they hire accountants, personnel managers and consultants. A shop steward should not expect, or be expected, to be all three. Any information should be questioned until it is understood.

Obtaining information

The recent experience of a group of shop stewards illustrates the importance of obtaining information.

As a condition of the acceptance of work study, the stewards had insisted that the information collected and prepared by the study engineers be made available to the stewards' committee. The first instalment of 'bumf' to come their way was a preliminary report based upon a general study which included 'activity sampling' (this particular technique is explained on page 22). The bulk of the report was relatively mundane, but, like most reports from consultants, the summary containing detailed estimates for the future was most revealing. This information enabled the stewards to calculate some of the probable gains their employer could expect from the introduction of work study and related incentive schemes.

Figure 1: *Summary of consultant's report*

Current situation

Time spent on unproductive work	=	30%
Time spent on waiting, delays, etc.	=	10%
Time spent on productive work	=	60%

The above figures had been obtained from the activity sampling exercise and, with the help of other preliminary observations, the consultant made the following estimates of what could be achieved through a detailed application of work study.

Proposed improvements

1 Unproductive time, which includes setting-up time and cleaning time, can be reduced to 20% of all available time.
2 Waiting time and delays can be reduced to 5% of all available time.
3 Revised methods of work can increase output by 10%.
4 Current work performance of operatives is estimated at 80% of standard performance. This can be raised to 100% of standard performance through the setting of realistic work standards and the introduction of an incentive scheme based on work measurement.

The above list shows how the consultant expected that productivity could be increased in two ways. The first was to reduce time spent on non-productive activities, delays and inefficient methods, and the second was to increase the actual pace of work. The stewards then tried some rough calculations to arrive at a general picture of how the consultant's four 'improvements' would affect current levels of output.

The first problem for the stewards was that the plant produced a variety of different products, and no two departments were really alike. Secondly, work tended to vary from day to day and the type of products could change from month to month. To overcome these problems they decided to calculate how the consultant's proposals would affect just **one person**; after all, the estimates were an average for the whole plant so why not 'invent' an average person? Whatever happened to the average person's productivity would be a fair indication of what would happen over the whole plant. The average person, they decided, would produce ten parts per hour (which for convenience we will call units) during each hour of uninterrupted work. Using the consultant's own figures for the current situation, the average person's output could be calculated as follows, assuming a 40-hour week:

Activity		Hours	Output
Unproductive work	30% =	12	nil
Waiting, delays	10% =	4	nil
Productive work	60% =	24 × 10 units =	240 units
	Total =	40 hours	

This meant that the stewards' hypothetical average person produced 240 units during an average 40-hour week, after allowing for the interruptions and delays which the consultant had suggested would normally occur.

This figure of 240 units per week then became the base from which to work out the increase in productivity to be expected from the consultant's four proposals. Figure 2 shows these calculations in detail.

Figure 2: *Shop stewards' calculations of increased productivity*

Current level of output per average 40 hours = 240 units

Proposals 1 and 2		Hours	Output
Unproductive time	*down* to 20% =	8	nil
Waiting time	*down* to 5% =	2	nil
Productive time	*up* to 75% =	30×10 units =	*300 units*
	Total =	*40 hours*	

Proposal 3
New methods of work which
increase productivity by 10%.
That is, output will rise
from the current 10 units per
hour to 11 units per hour = 30×11 units = *330 units*

Proposal 4
Increase average operative
performance from 80% of
standard to 100% of standard.
An increase of 20 points,
$^{20}/_{80} \times 100 = 25\%$. A 25% increase
raises hourly output from 11
units per hour to 13.75 $= \quad 30 \times 13.75$ units $= \textit{412.5 units}$

Summary

Current	= 240 units	
After proposals 1 & 2	= 300 units	$+25\%$
After proposal 3	= 330 units	$+37.5\%$ $+72\%$
After proposal 4	= 412.5 units	

The implementation of the consultant's proposals would be likely to
increase the overall level of productivity by 72%.

By simplifying the calculations in this way the stewards made
sense out of the information supplied and could present real
figures to the membership in an understandable form. Of course,
management could argue that not *everybody's* productivity will
rise by 72% and this is probably true. However, the calculations
were based upon estimates produced by the consultant to indicate
what could be achieved overall. As such, they would enable the
stewards to raise **fundamental** questions concerning the state of
the company's order book, and the prospects for expansion, shorter working time and a share of the savings.

The incentive scheme, when presented, is highly unlikely to
provide a 72% increase in pay. In fact most incentive schemes
based upon standard performance are unlikely to provide an
increase of more than 33%.

Part Two of this book discusses this type of bonus scheme in
detail and explains what is meant by 'standard performance'.

Activity sampling

The example described in the preceding pages mentioned the
consultant's use of activity sampling. This is a technique for estimating how time is actually spent. It is quite often used, especially
in workplaces which are being studied for the first time, to identify
areas of work which should be studied in greater detail later.
Relatively cheap and easy to apply, it can be used on all forms of

manual and clerical work. The technique is based upon the same theory as that used in opinion polls, namely that the intentions of a large number of people can be predicted with reasonable accuracy by taking a **sample** from a proportion of that larger group. Activity sampling is used to identify what workers are likely to be doing over a whole day or week, by taking a number of random samples (observations). Work study engineers will use one or two mathematical formulae for calculating the number of observations necessary to achieve a certain degree of accuracy. These formulae need not concern us here as they can be found in most work study textbooks. It is sufficient to say that, generally, an accuracy margin of plus or minus 2% is used.

The first step is to make a list of most of the activities which the study engineer would expect to occur over a normal working day or week. These activities are then allocated under two general headings, **'productive'** and **'non-productive'**. In work study jargon any activity which does not directly produce anything is termed 'non-productive', even if it is essential work. Taking a machine operative as an example, the sort of list of activities likely to be drafted by the study engineer is shown in Figure 3.

Figure 3: *Example of list of activities for use in activity sampling*

Productive work
1 machine running and work being produced

Non-productive work
2 setting-up
3 inspecting work
4 cleaning
5 talking to supervisor or shop steward
6 waiting for work
7 maintenance delay
8 other delay
9 absent from machine

The next steps are fairly simple and extremely tedious, which is why consultants often get local supervision to carry them out. Firstly, a programme of random times is drawn up using tables of random numbers produced by a computer. This programme of random times then becomes the sampler's schedule of visits to the area being studied. The sampler makes a note of the activity upon which each worker is engaged at each visit made in accordance with the schedule, until enough observations have been made to provide the required degree of accuracy. The total observations are then analysed as shown in Figure 4.

Figure 4: *Activity sampling − analysis of activities*

Activity	Observations	% of sample
1 productive work	1150	47.52
2 setting-up	120	4.96
3 inspecting work	60	2.48
4 cleaning	210	8.68
5 talking to supervision	20	.83
6 waiting for work	490	20.25
7 maintenance delay	140	5.79
8 other delay	80	3.31
9 absent from machine	150	6.20
Total	2420	

In the above example, from a total of 2420 observations management can estimate with a reasonable degree of accuracy that the machines in this particular department are producing for less than 50% of the time available. A glance at the analysis would suggest that management would probably wish to investigate the time spent 'waiting for work', 'cleaning', 'absent from machine' and lost through 'maintenance delay'.

Additional information can be obtained through the study engineer making an estimate of each worker's pace of work at the time of recording their activity. This is known as **'rated activity sampling'** and involves the rating technique which is discussed in Chapter 3. The rating figures are then averaged out across the recorded activities to produce an average effort rating for the department. It was this kind of survey which produced some of the information in the earlier example of a consultant's preliminary report.

The degree and scope of change which may be proposed as a result of method studies depends on the amount of money the employer is prepared to spend. If a great deal of capital is available for structural alterations and the purchase of new equipment, then a great deal of time and effort will be invested in method studies. Alternatively, if the employer has decided against substantial investment, consultants may limit themselves to seeking savings within the available budget. They will still carry out studies of existing patterns of work. They will use activity sampling and, inevitably, they will propose changes to established customs and practice.

Tasks and elements

When the employer is satisfied that the appropriate changes have been made to the general patterns of work, work flow, technology and staffing levels, the next step for the study engineer is to specify a **method of work** to be used for every task which is to be subsequently timed and measured. Workers usually think of themselves as being described by the job they perform – fitter, printer, driver, clerk, garment maker and so on. Study engineers are not remotely interested in these descriptions or the skills embodied within them. In fact they find such descriptions restrictive and a barrier to flexibility. Their job is to simplify work, to make it easier to study and easier to control. For these reasons, study engineers think of workers as performing a series of **tasks**, each of which can be separated from other tasks and each studied and timed.

Tasks

Almost any job can be simplified when it is broken down into a sequence of tasks. For example, observations may show that engineering workers spend their time in fetching and carrying, drawing parts from the stores, requisitioning tools, checking drawings and using a range of different types of machinery spread across the shop. After studying patterns of work in such a shop, the consultant might propose that: the general labouring work should be performed by somebody else (at a lower rate of pay); the use of certain machines should become the permanent job of one or two workers whose work is brought to them (specialisation); and, as specialisation would reduce the number of operations to be performed by any one worker, tools and gauges could be kept at the work station.

This would lead to work patterns more akin to the production line, where the workers' movements and range of work (and therefore skills) have been deliberately restricted.

A similar example may exist with clerical workers involved in typing, filing, maintaining records, calculating and making telephone calls – a wide range of tasks which could make study and overall control difficult. Investment in a word processor is likely to be accompanied by the proposed new job of 'word processor operator'. This avoids the cost of training everybody in the office to use the new machine and a job which formerly offered varied work and opportunities to socialise with colleagues becomes one of endless task repetition. The word processor operators may think that they produce letters and documents; the study engineer knows that they just punch keys.

The same approach is used when jobs contain elements of fault-finding or problem-solving. Mental work is non-productive and interferes with the main objective of producing. (It is also difficult to study and measure.) If at all possible, study engineers will propose that deductive thinking should be eliminated by simplifying the job or the product. Alternatively, they may propose that 'thinking work' should be allocated to one specific person, leaving the main group of workers to get on with the job in hand – producing. (It is no coincidence that manual workers are called 'hands'.) Once the range of tasks to be performed by a particular worker, or group of workers, has been identified, the study engineer will examine the sequence of movements and the tools and equipment involved and will then detail, step by step, the 'approved' method. 'Approved' by whom? is a reasonable question to ask. If union representatives are not involved at this stage the approval will lie solely with management.

Elements

In work study jargon the movements which constitute the task are called **'elements'**. Each element is clearly defined and will usually take between 3–25 seconds. Clearly, the fewer the tasks which make up a day's work, the easier it is for management to study, measure and control that particular worker.

Figure 5: *Example of a task separated into elements*

Task: assembling a battery-operated clock

Element description
1 pick up motor (left hand); pick up clock face (right hand); insert motor spindle through clock face.
2 pick up hour, minute and second hands (right hand); attach to spindle and locate at 12.
3 pick up locking nut (right hand) and screw to spindle.
4 place assembly on bench; pick up casing (left hand) and connect motor leads to battery compartment; solder (right hand).
5 fit casing to assembly.
6 fit hands adjuster to spindle at rear of casing and test.
7 pick up face cover (left hand) and fit to assembly.
8 place in plastic bag and box; place on conveyor.

The elements are selected and described by the study engineer for the convenience of the next operation – **measuring or timing the task**. It also ensures that the same elements are used by other study engineers. The example in Figure 5 shows a highly repetitive job where the work station would have been arranged so that all the necessary parts are at hand – this worker would need a good reason to be absent from his or her bench. Less repetitive tasks may not be described in such detail but will still be broken down into elements.

Arranging work into tasks and elements provides study engineers with their first defence against workers' attempts to confuse or mislead them. The Ford Motor Company's work standards training course, designed to give stewards an appreciation of work study, has almost nothing to say about method study, despite its benefits to management and the effects it may eventually have on work organisation. However, it does offer the following advice:

> If excessive motions are introduced by an operator, which affect the time for the element, the recording of such deviations from the prescribed method will be symbolised, circled and excluded from elemental time calculations. An explanation of the reason for disallowing the readings will be recorded. If an operator persists in using excessive motions during the observations, the study will be stopped for the foreman to reinstruct the operator in the prescribed method.

Although the extract mentions 'excessive motions' the same procedure would apply to the odd element which the operator might decide to throw in – perhaps making an 'unnecessary' measurement or inspection, taking 'excessive' care and attention, or making adjustments which are 'superfluous'. These will all be spotted as unnecessary padding when studies of the same task performed by different workers are compared. Likewise, other so-called unnecessary motions, such as nose blowing, head scratching and talking to workmates, will all be observed, recorded and eventually eliminated when task times are calculated.

Break points

One final refinement to the list of elements which make up a task is the addition of **'break points'**. A break point is simply a movement or moment which the engineer has decided denotes the end of one element and, therefore, the beginning of the next.

Break points will often be identified by clearly audible sounds, such as a machine starting or stopping, which are directly associated with the movement which ends the element.

Figure 6: *Example of elements and break points*

Part:	B.239 Gear case.	Drawing: 239/1
Material:	ISS 2 Cast iron.	
Operation:	Finish-mill second face.	
Machine:	No. 4 Cincinnati vertical miller.	
Fixture:	F. 239.	
Cutter:	25 cm. T.L.F.	
Gauge:	239/7. Surface plate.	

Elements and Break Points

A. Pick up casting, locate in fixture, lock two nuts, set guard, start machine and auto feed. Depth of cut 2.5 mm. Speed 80 r.p.m. Feed 40 cm/min.
    Break point: Machine commences cut.

B. Hold casting, break milled edge with file, clean with compressed air.
    Break point: Air gun dropped onto hook.

C. Move depth gauge to casting, check machined surface, move gauge away.
    Break point: Left hand releases gauge.

D. Pick up machined casting, carry to finished parts box and place aside, pick up next part and position on machine table.
    Break point: Casting hits table.

E. Wait for machine to complete cut.
    Break point: Machine ceases to cut.

F. Stop machine, return table, open guard, unlock fixture, remove machined casting and place on surface plate.
    Break point: Casting hits surface plate.

G. Clear swarf from machine table with compressed air.
    Break point: Air gun dropped onto hook.

Note: Elements B, C and D are inside work, and are performed on a casting which has already been machined while the milling machine is cutting the next casting. Element D includes bringing up into a handy position a fresh casting which will be machined after the one now in the machine.

Source: International Labour Office, *Introduction to Work Study* (revised edition), Geneva, 1977.

There is nothing particularly significant about break points except that they help the engineer to make the study, which can be a fairly stressful business involving the recording of elements, element times, effort rating, reading the stopwatch, identifying excessive motions and picking up unnecessary activities. Remembering that elements have an average duration of around ten seconds, it is helpful if some break points can be heard as well as seen.

Figure 6 shows an engineering task broken into elements with audible break points. Equipped with a list of elements and break points, the study engineer is ready to carry out a study. He or she knows almost precisely what to expect from the task to be studied; the unexpected will be recorded and subsequently scrutinised.

Trade unions have for too long allowed management to control and determine work methods. There seems to be some conventional wisdom that trade unions may bargain over job times and pay but work methods are for management to determine. The unfettered use of method study in the interests of employers has determined, and will continue to determine, the way in which workers spend half their conscious lives. Method study is not of itself inherently 'bad', nor does it inevitably produce results which are 'bad' for the worker. It is simply a technique, a systematic approach to studying work methods. It is the *purpose* behind the use of method study which determines the results.

When used by consultants and management on behalf of employers, the purpose is to reduce costs. There are countless reasons why methods should be studied, for example to make work less arduous, more interesting, safer and, even, enjoyable. However, while employers do not pick up the bill for a polluted environment, industrial disease and demented workers, the word 'costs' will continue to have a narrow definition.

Summary of Chapter 2

■ The **aims** of employers in using method study are to:
a) find out what actually goes on in the workplace at present;
b) use the information to propose new methods of working which may involve investment in new technology and redundancies;
c) simplify operations; and

    d) reduce or eliminate non-productive activities, such as delays, work customs, transportation of materials, movement of workers.

■ The overall objective is to produce information which can be used to reduce **costs**, including labour costs.

■ The information gained through method study is extremely useful to employers in day-to-day **negotiations** with trade unionists, irrespective of any future introduction of work measurement and incentive schemes.

■ The continual study and development of work methods in the interests of employers has led to the **erosion and disappearance of job skills**, the creation of boring, repetitive jobs and the existence of stress through the treatment of manual and clerical workers as units of energy rather than as human beings.

■ The introduction of new methods of work may be accompanied by new **health and safety hazards**, including stress.

■ Employers can achieve greater increases in productivity from the study of **existing methods** of work than can often be gained through work measurement and incentive schemes.

■ Where work measurement is to be subsequently applied, jobs are divided into **tasks** which are then sub-divided into **elements**. Elements are given **break points** for the convenience of study engineers.

■ The written sequence of elements which constitutes a particular task is clearly defined as a **defence** against workers' attempts to deceive.

■ Once established, only the **'approved'** method may be used.

Checklist on method study

■ Does your procedure agreement contain a clear **'status quo'** clause requiring any change in work methods to be **agreed** with the membership?

■ Have you negotiated an agreement which provides that all surveys, reports, studies and recommendations produced by study engineers, consultants and management must be **copied** to union representatives?

■ Does your agreement permit union representatives sufficient facilities and time during working hours to:

a) study the documentation?
b) discuss it with members?
c) hold meetings with members?
d) discuss it with other stewards or the stewards' committee?
e) discuss it with safety representatives?
f) hold the information in files to which union representatives have ready access?

■ Have you negotiated the right to be regularly supplied with **current** (that is, pre-work study) information on output, staffing, labour hours and costs so that you can **assess the effects** of proposed changes in work methods?

■ Does your agreement state that only those study methods **approved** by the membership may be used?

■ Does your agreement state that new work methods must eliminate **health and safety risks**, unnecessary **physical labour** and working conditions which **discriminate against women**?

■ Does your agreement require that new machinery and equipment must **improve** the working environment, feature best practice in ergonomic design and be utilised in a manner which does not produce boring or repetitive tasks, or the isolation of workers from their colleagues?

3.
Time study

What is time study? / recording time studies /
rating / facts, half-truths and statistics / summary /
checklist

Chapter 1 explained that there are usually two basic steps in
the application of work study: method study and work measurement. So far, we have looked at the way in which study engineers
approach a particular job with the objective of sub-dividing that
job into a series of tasks, each task being subsequently broken
down into a sequence of elements. This is part of the so-called
'scientific management' approach to the control of work and
assists employers in closely defining **what** is done and **how** it is
done. The next step is to define **how long** it takes to do it. This is
the purpose of **work measurement**.

Work can be measured in hundreds of different ways. All
workers have an output of some description whether it is tons of
coal mined, letters typed or patients treated. The simple measurement of output has one major drawback – how does one compare,
for example, digging a trench ten feet long by two feet wide and
three feet deep, with cleaning a large hospital ward? One thing
which all forms of output have in common is that they take time.
Measuring the time involved in performing a whole range of tasks
enables the output produced by each task to be compared or
assessed in one common unit of measurement – hours and minutes.

Of course, if that was all that interested employers it would be
a simple matter to get each worker to complete a daily time sheet
stating how he or she spent the time at work and how much was
produced. These records could then be checked by taking random
timings of the tasks being performed. However, data collected in
that way would simply inform management how long particular
jobs take *at the moment*, and the data would be heavily dependent
upon the speed at which workers chose to work and how often they
paused to rest. What the employer really wants to know is how
long each job *should* take, and this reflects not only the method of

work used but also the pace of work and the effort expended by the worker. Having sorted out the method of work the employer now needs to measure the time involved in each task and to make some judgement about the effort of the worker performing it.

What is time study?

Most systems of work measurement make use of the stop-watch and some type of effort rating. Time study uses both quite openly and is the key to understanding most other work measurement systems, even those like PMTS which appear not to use them at all. (PMTS stands for 'Pre-determined Motion Time Systems', a technique which is often sold to trade unionists on the false basis that it does not entail the use of the stopwatch or effort rating. See Chapter 6.)

Time study is a procedure for measuring work with the aid of stopwatch times which are then 'adjusted' to take account of the differing speeds at which the work is carried out. The objective is to set a **time for each task** which takes account of the pace of work, working conditions and the workers' need for rest – at least that's the theory. The task times are said to be those which are within the capability of the average experienced worker and are called **'standard times'**.

Having a catalogue of standard times for almost all tasks which are carried out in a particular workplace gives the employer much greater control over the enterprise's activities. Standard times can be used for job planning, delivery dates, costing, budgeting, scheduling work, planning labour and overtime and, perhaps, as the basis for incentive bonus schemes. It is important to see the use of standard times in that order of priority. Incentive schemes are merely a way of stimulating workers to co-operate with management planning and to meet objectives set by management. Where the pace of work is controlled by a machine or a production line, employers may see no need to introduce incentive schemes. Furthermore, certain political and economic conditions, such as the suppression of trade-union organisation or the creation of high levels of unemployment, may enable the employer to enlist alternative 'incentives'.

A standard time is not a clever invention which allows workers a method of calculating incentive bonus earnings; it represents the time within which the employer expects a task to be completed after taking account of the nature of the task and the vagaries of production and worker fatigue. In reality, the final standard time for any task depends upon a number of factors: what study engineers are allowed to get away with, management power, trade-union organisation and membership awareness. This chapter deals with time study in detail and particularly examines the opportunities for **negotiation** as opposed to bogus 'consultations' or unrestrained decision-making by consultants and management. The following two chapters explain how time study information is used to calculate standard times and the issues involved for union representatives.

Recording time studies

Once the study engineer is satisfied that the approved method is being used in the task to be studied, recordings with pencil and paper commence. The number of studies to be made, on whom they are made and their duration, will depend upon the study engineer's judgement – unless trade unionists have demanded the right to have a say in the matter. The engineer carrying out a study will note the following:

■ a description of the task;
■ each element performed;
■ the stopwatch timing for each element;
■ a judgement of the worker's speed and efficiency in performing each element; and
■ other incidents and activities which occur during the study.

The main aim is to record stopwatch times and ratings for those elements which are considered essential to the completion of the task, so that an average time for the task can be calculated. Usually, elements which are deemed to be essential fall into two main categories – **repetitive** elements and **occasional** elements. Repetitive elements are those which are a necessary part of the task and which occur every time the task is carried out. Occasional elements are also considered to be necessary work, but they occur occasionally or infrequently.

An hour's study is likely to record large numbers of repetitive elements, a much smaller number of occasional elements and a few other activities, such as minor delays, a visit to the toilet, mistakes and possibly the odd chat to the supervisor, shop steward or workmate. (Separating the various element recordings and dealing with the other activities is usually done in the work study office, away from questioning eyes on the shop floor.) During the study itself, the engineer is carrying out two main operations – recording selected **facts** (what happened and how long it took) and recording **opinion** (his or her judgement of the worker's pace of working).

The stopwatch recording for each element is usually known as the **'observed time'**. (These labels are important because the recorded time goes through three stages of adjustment and each stage has its own label.) Observed times are always recorded in decimal minutes which means that each minute on the stopwatch is divided into hundredths of a minute instead of seconds. A reading on a normal watch of fifteen seconds will show on a decimal stopwatch as .25 minutes (a quarter of a minute).

Engineers using traditional, wind-up stopwatches can choose between **'flyback'** timing and **'continuous'** timing. With **flyback** timing, the watch reading is taken at the end of each element and a button is depressed which causes the sweep hand to fly back to zero. This method has the advantage of producing a separate observed time for each element. However, some study engineers believe that flyback timing is responsible for watch reading errors and they prefer the continuous recording method. In **continuous** recording the flyback button is not used at the end of each element; instead the sweep hand is allowed to tick on continuously and the watch reading is recorded at the end of each element. The disadvantage of the latter method is that the time for each element has to be calculated later by deducting each element time from the following element time.

The choice of methods is not particularly important and certainly not an issue to be too concerned about. With modern quartz digital timers, all sorts of options are available, many of which are only really suitable for highly repetitive work. Claims that quartz timers make time study easier are often over-stated and most work study practitioners will stick to the trusty stopwatch. Irrespective of the technology, the objective is to record observed times and ratings for subsequent analysis.

The actual study **sheets**, upon which the engineer records the elements, activities, ratings and observed times, vary from one employer to another and from one firm of consultants to another.

Figure 7: *Example of a study sheet recording elements and activities in chronological order*

element	OT	R	BT	element	OT	R	BT
A	·17	90	·15	A	·15	100	·15
B	·80		·80	B	·81		·81
C	·22	90	·20	C	·20	95	·19
D	·10	100	·10	D	·10	95	·10
E	·30	100	·30	E	·32	95	·31
F	·13	90	·12	F	·13	95	·12
A	·16	95	·15	visit toilet and talk to steward	5·27		
B	·82		·82	A	·18	90	·16
C	·20	100	·20	B	·80		·80
D	·09	110	·10	C	·22	90	·20
E	·26	110	·29	D	·11	90	·10
F	·10	110	·11	E	·33	90	·30
adjust m/c setting	·25	100	·25	F	·15	85	·1
A	·12	115	·14	A	·22		
B	·82		·82	B			
C	·16	115	·18	C			
D	·08	115	·09	D			
E	·27	110	·30				
F	·12	100	·12				

OT=observed time   R=rating   BT=basic time

Figure 8: *Example of a study sheet with identical elements grouped for easier recording*

element code	description		1	2	3	4	5	6	7
A	Pick up casting and locate in machine	OT	·17	·16	·12	·15	·18	·22	
		R	90	95	115	100	90	85	
		BT	·15	·15	·14	·15	·16	·19	
B	Machine milling	OT	·60	·82	·82	·81	·80	·81	
		R							
		BT	·80	·82	·82	·81	·80	·81	
C	Remove finished casting — clean with compressed air	OT	·22	·20	·16	·20	·22	·24	
		R	90	·100	115	95	90	85	
		BT	·20	·20	·18	·19	·20	·20	
D	Check with gauge	OT	·10	·09	·08	·10	·11	·14	
		R	·100	110	110	95	90	90	
		BT	·10	·10	·09	·10	·10	·11	
E	File edge, clean and place in box	OT	·30	·26	·27	·32	·33	·37	
		R	100	110	110	95	90	90	
		BT	·30	·29	·30	·31	·30	·33	
F	Clean machine with compressed air	OT	·13	·10	·12	·13	·15	·13	
		R	90	110	100	95	85	90	
		BT	·12	·11	·12	·12	·13	·12	

Note: The first sequence of elements, ABCDEF, is read vertically in column 1, the second in column 2 and so on. Basic times are added after the study is completed.

Some sheets are designed so that the study engineer records each element, its rating and observed time on one line, the next element as it occurs on the line immediately below, and the next on the line below that, and so on. A lot of paper gets used this way but the finished sheets do have the advantage of showing, in chronological order, each activity as it occurred during the study. This is advantageous to union representatives who wish to check the study at a later date, as it shows up minor delays and interruptions.

A second type of study sheet is favoured for recording highly repetitive tasks, where the study engineer expects to see the same sequence of elements carried out over and over again with little divergence or interruption. This type of sheet enables the engineer to write out the sequence of elements in advance, and allows up to ten recordings of each element to be made on one line. In this case the finished study sheets condense all the information about repetitive elements together, but as long as all the relevant information about delays and interruptions is also recorded, the choice of study sheets is often a matter of style. The issue for union representatives is 'whose style'? It is far more important that the membership can understand the recordings made of their work than to have recordings made in the style which suits the study engineer. Figures 7 and 8 show examples of the two types of study sheet mentioned above.

Rating

Earlier I mentioned that itemising the method of work, element by element, provided study engineers with their first line of defence against workers who attempt to introduce the odd 'unnecessary' element or activity. 'Rating' is their second line of defence against those who attempt to achieve the same result by going slow. Rating allows study engineers to adjust the observed times recorded on the stopwatch to take account of the worker's pace of working. In effect, this means that times recorded on slow workers will be adjusted downwards, and times recorded on fast workers will be adjusted upwards.

Rating is entirely a matter of opinion and, for this reason, has been one of the most controversial aspects of time study. It relies entirely upon the study engineer's mental picture of what is called **'standard rating'**, that is, a pace of work which is considered to be fair and reasonable. What is 'fair and reasonable' is clearly a subjective judgement depending upon where you stand in the employment relationship. In many cases, 'fair and reasonable' is interpreted through negotiations over output levels and rest breaks, etc. between unions and employers. Rating is an attempt to place this interpretation completely in the hands of the employer. To my knowledge, none of the rating scales in use today was drawn up in consultation or negotiation with workers.

The judgement which the study engineer has to make is whether a prticular worker's pace of work is at standard rating, below standard or above standard. To do this a rating scale is used: standard rating is given a figure of 100; if a worker's pace of work is judged to be just below standard then a rating of 95 or 90 may be recorded. Similarly, if the pace of work is judged to be faster than standard, a rating of 105 or 110 may be given. Usually, the range of ratings recorded during a study will be between 75 and 125. In conventional time study, every element recorded will be given a separate rating, which means that the study engineer has to exercise his or her judgement every ten seconds or so. Consultants, experts and work study practitioners can never *prove* that a particular pace of work is standard; nor, on the other hand, can their opinion about a worker's efforts be *disproved* – it's a bit like arguing whether a carpet is bluey-green or greeny-blue.

Of course, the experts will say that rating is a skill for which they have been highly trained and it may be an amusing diversion for stewards to inquire as to the content of this 'skill training'. It usually consists of showing short films of workers performing tasks at varying speeds while our would-be 'experts' are invited to rate each task shown. The budding practitioner is deemed to have passed this test when his or her judgements coincide consistently with the opinions of the group of experts who made the film in the first place.

In his book on productivity deals, Tony Cliff quotes the example of a rating experiment involving 24 time study engineers, each of whom was invited to observe and rate three tasks. The results showed that the study engineers who had received similar training recorded variations across the group of up to 32%. The variations between observers with different training was as high as 76%. (Tony Cliff, *The Employers' Offensive*, Pluto Press, London, 1970, pp. 103, 104.)

The problem for trade unionists is that while rating is just a matter of **opinion**, it is as important in working out the final job time as the original observed time which, remember, was a recorded **fact**. Observed times are adjusted by the rating figure to produce what are called **'basic times'**. This adjustment is calculated after the study has been completed, using the following formula:

$$\text{observed time} \times \frac{\text{rating}}{100} = \text{basic time}$$

Figure 9 shows how this formula works in practice.

Figure 9: *Examples of basic time calculations*

Observed time	Rating			Basic time
.50 minutes	80	$(.50 \times \frac{80}{100})$	=	.40 minutes
.50 minutes	100	$(.50 \times \frac{100}{100})$	=	.50 minutes
.50 minutes	120	$(.50 \times \frac{120}{100})$	=	.60 minutes
.20 minutes	90	$(.20 \times \frac{90}{100})$	=	.18 minutes
.20 minutes	110	$(.20 \times \frac{110}{100})$	=	.22 minutes

The examples clearly show that low ratings produce low basic times which will ultimately produce job times often described as 'tight'. Having recorded all the repetitive elements along with the occasional elements and other activities which occurred during the study, the study engineer then converts all the observed times into basic times using the rating factor recorded during the study. Observed times are now discarded and the artificially-adjusted basic times (all now at standard rating) are assembled to calculate a 'standard time' for the task.

One other rating issue which will have to be considered is the treatment to be given to elements which are virtually impossible to rate, for example those which are totally machine-controlled. The machine operates under power and the operative is unable to influence or adjust its speed. A conventional wisdom, and one usually accepted by trade unions, is that the actual observed times for machine-controlled elements are used as basic times with no interference through rating. (In fact, this is the same as rating all machine-controlled elements at 100.) However, agreements have been signed which allow machine elements to be rated below 100 – as low as 75 in some cases. On the other hand, stewards in some plants have succeeded in convincing management that machine

elements are neutral and should be rated in line with the operative's own average pace of work. This is fine if you work at 100 or
more but no so helpful if your average rating is below 100. Either
way an agreement to rate machine elements at the worker's average pace of working still leaves a lot of control in the hands of the
study engineer who decides the average rating in the first place.

By allowing machine elements to be rated below 100, management are effectively saying that although the time for the
element is controlled by machine, the time allowed will be less
than the time it actually takes!

A similar argument can be applied to other elements which
defy the study engineer's 'skill', such as inspections, and the giving
and receiving of instructions. The engineer cannot really say that
the worker's eyes, mouth or tongue should have moved faster or
that fewer words could have been used in communicating (although given the chance there are some who would attempt it).
Again, the conventional wisdom is to treat the observed times as
basic times for such elements. These issues need to be clarified
from the start if rating is to be used.

One final point on rating concerns the rating scale which the
study engineer uses. Throughout this section we have concentrated on the scale which expresses standard at 100. This is the
British Standards Institution (BSI) rating scale which is the most
widely used in Britain. Others include the Bedaux 60–80 scale,
which gives standard a figure of 80, and the 100–133 scale which
puts standard at 133. There is no need to be confused by these
variations, particularly as the latter two scales are in declining use,
and a comparison with more familiar units, speed limits for example, will make it clear. A limit of 30 miles per hour would show
as 48 kilometres an hour on a metric speedometer – the speed is
the same but the figures are different.

At one time, each of these scales placed an emphasis, not only
on standard rating, but also upon **'normal rating'**, normal rating
being the pace of work expected from an 'unmotivated' worker
and standard the pace of a 'motivated' worker. This now outdated
concept of 'normal' performance can sometimes be useful to bear
in mind when negotiating over the introduction of incentive
schemes. We will return to it in the chapters on incentives. However, it is enough to point out at this stage that, whatever the rating
scale in use, 'standard' is a pace of work requiring one-third
greater effort than 'normal', as the following table shows.

Figure 10: *Comparison of three rating scales*

Rating scale	'Normal'		'Standard'
BSI 0–100	75	increase	100
100–133	100 ⟶	one-third ⟶	133
Bedaux 60–80	60	(33%)	80

The rating scales in Figure 11 illustrate this relationship further, and give examples and descriptions of various levels of effort which work study experts consider appropriate. Standard (100), for example, is quoted as being equivalent to walking at four miles per hour under ideal conditions. This, of course, is not a complex scientific illustration nor does it represent the outcome of years of negotiations between employers and trade unions – it is a concept which has been imposed by employers and their advisers.

Facts, half-truths and statistics

On one or two occasions in this chapter, I have referred to the activities and observed times recorded on the study sheet, as **facts**. Assuming that the study engineer is reasonably honest, this will usually be the case. However, it does not necessarily follow that *all* the facts will be recorded; statistics are compiled by selecting certain facts and omitting others. Soccer players are said to have no more than 60 to 120 seconds' actual contact with the ball during a match – a fact. This simple statement of fact does nothing to convey the amount of running, covering, marking and tackling which that same player may have to do during the course of the game.

Similarly, a time study narrowly focussed on 'essential' work may well miss a lot of the to-ing and fro-ing which is necessary to maintain output. Oversights of this nature can also occur if the study is too short, or if production has been carefully 'set up' to run smoothly. It's not just the members who may feel under pressure or on trial when a study is being made; supervisors often feel that way too. The result can often be that the fastest workers, the best machines and the peak production periods are those which are studied, with supervisors scurrying around to make sure that everything is 'ready' for the appearance of the study engineer.

Figure 11: *Rating scales and descriptions*

Scales			Description	Comparable walking speed	
60–80	100–133	0–100 Standard		(mph)	(km/h)
0	0	**0**	No activity.		
40	67	**50**	Very slow; clumsy, fumbling movements; operator appears half asleep, with no interest in the job.	2	3.2
60	100	**75**	Steady, deliberate, unhurried performance, as of a worker not on piecework but under proper supervision; looks slow, but time is not being intentionally wasted while under observation.	3	4.8
80	133	**100 (standard rating)**	Brisk, businesslike performance, as of an average qualified worker on piecework; necessary standard of quality and accuracy achieved with confidence.	4	6.4
100	167	**125**	Very fast; operator exhibits a high degree of assurance, dexterity and co-ordination of movement, well above that of an average trained worker.	5	8.0
120	200	**150**	Exceptionally fast; requires intense effort and concentration, and is unlikely to be kept up for long periods; a 'virtuoso' performance only achieved by a few outstanding workers.	6	9.6

Source: Adapted from the International Labour Office, *Introduction to Work Study* (revised edition), Geneva, 1977.

During the study they will try their best to avoid distracting the operatives while attempting to remove obstacles, make adjustments and generally keep the whole operation running smoothly.

This is not to suggest that supervisors are hand-in-glove with the study engineers to perpetrate some kind of conspiracy upon the workers, although the end result may arouse suspicions of that nature. This behaviour is more likely to be the effect of being studied and watched. It has similar effects on manual and clerical workers, who tend to speed up. One way to prevent or reduce this tendency is to ensure that the membership is properly briefed about the purpose of the study and the type of information to be recorded. A similar discussion with local supervisors and their representatives may help to produce a common understanding and one or two agreed ground rules.

Selecting the times at which studies are made and the circumstances under which they are made will affect the statistics produced. Very short studies may well overlook the occasional work which is a necessary part of the job. Removing finished products, drawing supplies, checking quality, adjusting machines or equipment, are typical examples. If these are overlooked or deliberately excluded, the eventual job time will be tight.

Selecting the workers to be studied can be of similar importance although, under the conventions of work study, only 'qualified' workers are supposed to be studied. The term qualified eliminates learners and apprentices but, loosely applied, could also screen out the older and slower workers. In any group of workers there will always be those management prefer, because of their attitude, temperament and physique; 'trouble-makers', 'militants' and 'perfectionists' may be avoided, along with the old-timer performing on a badly-maintained machine at 8.30 on Monday morning.

The only effective way for union representatives to check on these factors is to get the membership involved by keeping them informed. Every members should be on the alert for anything unusual, and willing to feed information back to his or her steward. Similarly, stewards need to avoid acting in isolation by regularly exchanging news and views.

Summary of Chapter 3

■ Time studies are carried out by direct observation of **'qualified'** workers working to the **'approved'** method for each task.
■ The purpose of the study is to record:
  a) all the elements necessary for the completion of the task;
  b) an observed time for each element;
  c) a rating for each element; and
  d) any other activities.
■ Rating is the subjective judgement of the study engineer; it cannot be correct or incorrect, it is an **opinion** as valid as the opinion of the union representative or worker concerned.
■ Observed times are recorded in hundredths of a minute (**decimal minutes**).
■ After the study is completed, observed times are converted into basic times by using the **rating factor**. (This step is sometimes called 'extending the study'.)
■ **Machine-controlled** elements are usually rated at 100, so that the basic time is the same as the observed time. However, this cannot be guaranteed and may be a matter for negotiation.
■ The **number** of studies made, their **duration**, **when** they are made, and **who** is studied are all important issues – too important to be left to management and study engineers alone to decide.

Checklist on time study

■ Does your agreement state that all methods of work measurement must first be **approved** by the membership?
■ Does the agreement provide that the following must be **mutually agreed**:
  a) the 'approved' method of work?
  b) the definition of a 'qualified worker'?
  c) the number, duration and timing of studies?
■ Have your members agreed to the use of **rating**? Have you considered alternatives, such as not using rating at all and using **average** observed times instead?
■ Have you the right to **challenge** ratings?
■ What treatment has been agreed for **machine-controlled** elements?

■ Will union representatives automatically receive **copies** of all studies carried out on their members?

■ Have facilities been provided for union representatives to **examine**, **discuss** and **file** copies of studies?

■ Have union representatives the right to **reject** studies? (It should be remembered that employers and consultants always have this right – they simply tear them up.)

■ Do union representatives have the right to **watch** time studies being carried out? (In particular, watch out for the manipulation of working conditions to produce an 'ideal' workflow, and for unusual 'assistance' from supervision.)

4.
Analysing time study information

Analysing time study information / organising time study information / re-cap / summary / checklist

In far too many cases, study engineers, after completing their observations, simply return to the relative peace and quiet of their office to organise, analyse and summaries the information they have collected. Some time later, they emerge to present workers and their representatives with a slip of paper upon which is written the standard time for the task they have studied. Between these two points – completing the studies and issuing a standard time – they have the opportunity to make a wide range of decisions, untroubled by questions and objections from union representatives and unfettered by the niceties of negotiations.

Of course, management will be able to influence these decisions at any time but, if workers and their representatives are unaware of the issues, the interests of the members will hardly be considered. The decisions referred to concern the treatment of information recorded during the studies and the allocation of various allowances to cover rest and fatigue.

All too often collective agreements on work study fail to give union representatives the right of involvement in these decisions. The result is complete management control. This chapter examines the first stage in calculating the standard time for a task.

Organising time study information

After converting observed times into basic times, the study engineer needs to organise the information recorded during the study into a more readily usable form. Starting with the repetitive elements contained in the task, the basic times for each element are totalled and an average basic time for each element calculated. This is a simple and straightforward operation, as shown by the example in Figure 12, using the recordings from Figure 7 on page 36.

Figure 12: *Calculating an average basic time for repetitive elements*

	Basic times				
Element A: .15	.15	.14	.15	.16	.19
Total basic minutes:					.94 mins
Divide by number of observations:					6
Average basic time:					.16 mins

Normally, more than six observations would be required to get a reasonable sample, although it is not uncommon in some industries for study engineers to issue a standard time on the flimsiest of studies. Note also that the sixth basic time for element A is considerably longer than the pattern shown in the remaining five; in many cases the study engineer will 'circle out' any abnormally high or low times and disregard them in all subsequent calculations. In this example, if the sixth observation was disregarded, the average basic time for element A would fall from .16 minutes to .15 minutes. This is one good reason why union representatives should see the study engineer's calculations.

Again, using the figures from the example on page 36, the average basic times for the repetitive elements in the task are calculated in the same way, as shown in Figure 13.

Figure 13: *Calculating the total average basic time for all repetitive elements in the task*

Element	Basic times						Total basic mins	No. of obs	Average basic time
A	.15	.15	.14	.15	.16	.19	.94	6	.16
B	.80	.82	.82	.81	.80	.81	4.86	6	.81
C	.20	.20	.18	.19	.20	.20	1.17	6	.20
D	.10	.10	.09	.10	.10	.11	.60	6	.10
E	.30	.29	.30	.31	.30	.33	1.83	6	.31
F	.12	.11	.12	.12	.13	.12	.72	6	.12
								Total	1.70

The study engineer now has an average basic time of 1.7 minutes for all the repetitive elements involved in completing that particular task. In some industries or plants, where trade-union organisation is weak, this statistic is all the employer will want to use. Add, say, a 10% allowance for fatigue and personal needs, and the standard time for the task can be issued as: 1.7 minutes plus 10% = 1.87 minutes. This is not to suggest that all employers and work study practitioners are as unscrupulous as that. The employer, however, *is* paying the consultant's fees and, given the opportunity, they will cut job times as far as is possible.

The procedure we have just looked at takes no account of occasional elements. It is only part of the picture. The engineering worker in the example may be required to draw new parts at various times, take away completed parts, or make adjustments to the machine. A garment maker operating a sewing machine will periodically have to insert a new reel of thread or obtain a fresh supply of buttons, and so on. Both of them may have to make occasional detailed inspections of the work they are producing (after all, they have to take responsibility for it). Both may need to talk to – and listen to – their supervisors. In almost any job, there will be countless minor diversions and incidents which must be either covered by the standard time for the task or negotiated separately. Of course employers want work study to eliminate these unproductive occurrences where possible. Where they succeed completely you have automatons instead of human beings, hands but not brains, with the real robots themselves not far behind.

Occasional elements and activities are covered either by negotiation or by calculations based upon the information recorded in the studies. As an example, assume that during the studies of the milling operation shown on page 37, the occasional element 'adjust machine setting' was observed and recorded five times, and that the average basic time for this element was .24 minutes. The study engineer now knows that every so often the string of repetitive elements (sometimes called the work cycle) is interrupted by an occasional need to adjust the machine setting and that this operation takes .24 minutes on average. As the adjustment does not occur in each and every work cycle, all that needs to be done is to find the frequency or **rate** at which it occurs over a period. This can be calculated by going back to the study sheets to find how many work cycles were completed during the studies; assuming that 40 work cycles were observed, the simple calculation shown in Figure 14 can be made.

Figure 14: *Calculating the allocation of time for occasional elements*

Occasional element: 'adjust machine setting'
Basic times: .24   .22   .27   .24   .23
Number of observations: 5
Average basic time: .24 minutes
Number of work cycles in study: 40
Rate of occurrence: 5 in 40 = 1 in 8
Proportion of occasional
element to be allocated to
the work cycle time: one-eighth of .24 minutes
                                 = .03 minutes

Just under two seconds (.03 minutes) can now be allocated to the basic time for the work cycle to cover the occasional need to adjust the machine setting.

Similar treatment can be given to other occasional activities, so what is the problem? There are probably three issues here:

a) if the studies are short, the occasional activities **may not be recorded** at all;

b) if they are recorded, there is nothing to stop the study engineer from **ignoring** them; and

c) where they are noticed but not recorded, management may try to insist that such activities are **unnecessary** and constitute what is called 'ineffective time'.

Clearly, union representatives need to be vigilant in checking which activities are included and which excluded from the calculations and this is bound to entail taking advice from the members concerned.

All kinds of irregular activities may occur and be recorded during a time study. Other than repetitive elements which *always* occur during the work cycle, they can be broadly covered under the following headings: **occasional elements; ineffective time; and contingencies.**

Occasional elements

Occasional elements are generally regarded as activities which are useful work and necessary to the job in hand. Some of the examples used in this section are typical of occasional elements – adjusting machinery, drawing new materials, checking work and so on. Some work study manuals include such activities as 'taking or giving instructions' and 'answering the telephone'. Even so, there is still ample room for argument and it is a useful starting point for union representatives to assume that any activity which occurs **occasionally** and which involves some kind of **work** is an occasional element.

Ineffective time

As a broad rule of thumb, any time recorded during the study as waiting – waiting for work, for instructions, for materials, etc. – will be discarded from the study calculations as ineffective time. The reasoning is simple; the aim of work measurement is to produce a standard time for a particular task or work cycle which a qualified worker can achieve repeatedly over the whole day or shift. Waiting time is an inefficiency (probably management's) which management will attempt to eliminate. If ineffective time is built into the standard time then work measurement is merely helping to perpetuate inefficiencies. Union representatives may well be outraged by such management logic, and will probably demand to know what happens to their members' bonus earnings when waiting time occurs. Again, it must be remembered that standard times are produced primarily to assist management planning and costing, not to settle bonus issues.

In fact, it is far better for union representatives to allow waiting time to be dealt with as ineffective time and to tackle the issue of bonus earnings in relation to waiting time as a completely separate issue. In the long run, more protection is afforded by clear agreements on payment for waiting time and other delays, than by attempts to include some allowance in the standard time. For example, if waiting time increases, what was a reasonable allowance last year may be totally inadequate this year.

The exception to this approach is when waiting time is an unavoidable and necessary part of the work cycle, such as waiting for a machine to stop so that the next manual element can be carried out. This is not really waiting time at all, but part of a machine-controlled element.

Any recordings of workers taking rests, going to the toilet or washing will be dismissed from the study as ineffective time. These activities are regarded as relaxation and are dealt with when allocating allowances for rest and personal needs. This does not mean that all activities designated as ineffective can be ignored. Employers will often take a very narrow view of what is 'necessary' to the task in hand and reject activities which union representatives consider necessary. This is a further reason why study documentation should be scrutinised; it would be particularly helpful if study engineers were compelled to list each activity which they have designated as ineffective, on a separate part of the study sheets.

Contingencies

Contingencies tend to be a dustbin of odd items which are neither occasional elements nor ineffective time. Some companies adopt the policy of advocating a fixed percentage allowance in all standard times to cover all minor delays and incidents. Examples would be cotton breaks on sewing machines, or rejecting faulty parts or materials. The list is potentially endless. Contingency allowances are supposed to cover all minor and short duration interruptions. In reality they seldom do. For example, one agreement in the public sector suggests that a contingency allowance of 5% is intended to cover all delays of less than 30 minutes' duration. In practice, this means that the workers concerned cannot book any delays unless they exceed 30 minutes. But 5% of 40 hours is 2 hours; and 12 delays of 10 minutes each over the whole working week would exhaust the allowance completely, as would 4 delays of half an hour each.

Specific advice on this issue is difficult to offer as circumstances vary considerably from industry to industry and from occupation to occupation. However, if contingency allowances are calculated as so many minutes per shift or per week, union representatives are in a better position to assess what management is offering (if anything). For example, taking a normal working day as 480 minutes, a 10% contingency allowance would provide 48 minutes to cover minor delays, and a 4% allowance would provide 19 minutes. If management are then required to state all the occurrences which the allowance is intended to cover, the members have enough evidence to decide whether or not it is acceptable.

Management may suggest making a continuous study over one or two weeks to log everything which happens, as one way of making a check on the suitability of the contingency allowance. This is quite time-consuming and a majority of the membership may well object to the idea.

Re-cap

It is worth pausing at this stage to check on what the study engineer has achieved through analysing all the information recorded during the study of just one task. Continuing with the example used in Figure 13 and assuming three occasional elements as being agreed between unions and management, the build-up of the work cycle could now look something like Figure 15.

Figure 15: *Build-up of the basic time for the complete task or work cycle*

Repetitive element	A	.16 basic minutes	
Repetitive element	B	.81 basic minutes	
Repetitive element	C	.20 basic minutes	
Repetitive element	D	.10 basic minutes	Total 1.7
Repetitive element	E	.31 basic minutes	
Repetitive element	F	.12 basic minutes	
Occasional element	1	.03 basic minutes	
Occasional element	2	.04 basic minutes	Total .19
Occasional element	3	.12 basic minutes	
Contingency allowance		5%	

The total time for repetitive elements is 1.7 minutes to which has to be added .19 minutes for the calculated proportion of the three agreed occasional elements.

The contingency allowance is usually calculated as a proportion of the total basic minutes for repetitive elements. This gives a total basic time for the task of 1.7 minutes plus .19 minutes plus .085 minutes (5% of 1.7), which is 1.975 basic minutes.

The next step is to allocate allowances for rest and personal needs, and so convert the **basic time** above into the **standard time**.

Summary of Chapter 4

■ The basic times recorded for each element are totalled and divided by the number of observations of that element, to calculate an **average basic time** for the element.

■ Abnormally high or low times may be 'circled out', that is, **deleted**.

■ **Occasional elements** are apportioned according to the frequency with which they occur over a number of work cycles. A proportion of the average basic time for each occasional element is then added to the overall basic time for the work cycle.

■ A **contingency allowance** may be agreed to cover minor occurrences.

■ Some activities may be categorised as **'ineffective time'**, in which case study engineers will disregard them in all calculations.

■ The value of work study as a means of providing information to assist management control is now abundantly clear. At this stage of the procedure, written information has been collected which covers:

　　a) a detailed description of all the necessary **elements** which make up the work cycle;
　　b) a description of the **tools** and **materials** used;
　　c) an estimate of **how long** each element should take to perform;
　　d) a **description** and **frequency** of occurrence for all other activities; and
　　e) recordings of **time** spent on other activities.

Checklist on time study information

■ Does your agreement provide for all time study summaries to be **submitted** to union representatives?

■ Have facilities been provided to allow union representatives to **question** the study engineer and to **discuss** the documentation with members?

■ Will the study engineer be required to **justify** the reasons for categorising certain activities as **'ineffective'**?

■ Is the categorisation of **non-repetitive elements** subject to union approval?

■ Were the studies carried out over a representative period of **normal working conditions**?

■ Is it agreed that **contingency allowances** are subject to negotiation?

■ Check the **small print** – what is the contingency allowance intended to cover?

5.
Allowances and standard times

Allowances and machine elements / standard
times / policy allowances / summary / checklist

Allowances for rest – often called 'relaxation allowances' –
are added to the basic time for each element to compensate for
fatigue, personal needs and working conditions. Once allowances
have been added to the basic time for each element, it becomes the
standard time. So, to re-cap, the procedure for calculating standard times from stopwatch readings is:

observed time = stopwatch reading
basic time = stopwatch reading multiplied by rating factor
standard time = basic time plus allowances.

It is important to remember that the standard time could be
greater or smaller than the original observed time – it depends
entirely upon the study engineer's rating and the amount of allowances negotiated. The allocation of allowances can be as controversial as rating. It is another issue which is presented to workers
as being 'scientific'. Consultants and study engineers will produce
tables and charts to 'prove' that the appropriate allowance for
noisy conditions is 1%, for bending and stooping 2%, for lifting a
two-pound weight, nil, and so on.

Negotiating over allowances is like negotiating over pay – the
union asks for £10, the employer offers £6 and agreement is
reached somewhere in between. Unfortunately the similarity is
not quite that close because union representatives are seldom
aware that these items are negotiable at all. Often they react as
though allowances were evidence of humanitarian kindness on the
part of management.

Allowance tables have been dressed up in pseudo-scientific trappings, to make them seem more sophisticated. Consultants employ all the usual subtleties one might expect: 2% becomes 2.4% as though a decimal point here or there testifies to their scientific accuracy. Some consultants produce graphs and complex points systems which lead union representatives into bogus 'participation' in determining allowances, when the outcome has already been pre-arranged by the consultant who invented the graphs and tables.

Allowances are basically **time off** – time to stop work and blow your nose, go to the toilet or behave like a human being – and it pays to think of them in that way. The average relaxation allowance given across industry will lie somewhere between 12–20%. The workplaces at the top of that range will be those where the membership has insisted upon the right to negotiate allowances as opposed to having them determined in the work study office.

According to the conventional use of allowances, there are two kinds: a **constant** allowance which is supposed to cover fatigue and personal needs and which is always given, even on the least physical job; and, a **variable** allowance which is intended to cover certain types of working conditions. Even under the ILO tables, shown in Figure 16, the minimum allowance which can be given for work performed under ideal conditions whilst seated is 9%. Yet, all too often, employers have succeeded in getting lower allowances accepted, probably because trade unionists have been unaware of the issues involved. The Ford Motor Company's work standards training course states that the personal relief allowance for line-controlled operations is 40 minutes per eight-hour shift, including tea breaks. On other operations it is 28 minutes, including tea breaks. These allowances work out at 8.3% and 5.8% respectively.

Figure 16: *Typical table of relaxation allowances*

1. *CONSTANT ALLOWANCES:*	*percentages*	
	Men	Women
Personal Needs Allowance	5	7
Basic Fatigue Allowance	4	4
	9	11

2. *VARIABLE ADDITIONS TO BASIC FATIGUE ALLOWANCE*

A. Standing Allowance	2	4

B. Abnormal Position Allowance *percentages*

Slightly awkward	0	1
Awkward (bending)	2	3
Very awkward (lying, stretching up)	7	7

C. Weightlifting or Use of Force
(lifting, pulling or pushing)
Weight lifted or force exerted (in kg)

2.5	0	1
5	1	2
7.5	2	3
10	3	4
12.5	4	6
15	6	9
17.5	8	12
20	10	15
22.5	12	18
25	14	—
30	19	—
40	33	—
50	58	—

D. Light Conditions

Slightly below recommended value	0	0
Well below	2	2
Quite inadequate	5	5

E. Air Conditions *(excluding climatic features)*

Well ventilated, or fresh air	0	0
Badly ventilated, but no toxic or injurious fumes	5	5
Work close to furnaces, etc.	5–15	5–15

F. Visual Strain

Fairly fine work	0	0
Fine or exacting	2	2
Very fine or very exacting	5	5

G. Aural Strain

Continuous	0	0
Intermittent, loud	2	2
Intermittent, very loud High-pitched, loud	5	5

H. Mental Strain

Fairly complex process	1	1
Complex or wide span of attention	4	4
Very complex	8	8

I. Monotony: Mental

Low	0	0
Medium	1	1
High	4	4

J. Monotony: Physical

Rather tedious	0	0
Tedious	2	1
Very tedious	5	2

Source: International Labour Office, *Introduction to Work Study* (revised edition), Geneva, 1977.

The most rigorous system of applying allowances is to allocate them element by element through the work cycle. This means that each element is examined to see if it involves standing, lifting, abnormal posture, etc. This is not only time-consuming but difficult for any intelligent person to do without becoming nauseated by the dehumanising approach to work, which is inherent in work study.

Probably the least disruptive and most rewarding method (in more ways than one) is for all union representatives to establish a **joint policy** on allowances to put before the membership. This not only prevents divisions on the union side but also ensures that any complex systems presented by employers or consultants can be confidently handed back. A union policy on allowances could propose one single figure across the board (say 20%).

On the other hand, working conditions may **vary** considerably between departments, in which case allowances could be set to reflect those variations. But the issue of working conditions needs to be approached with some caution; negotiating an extra percentage here and there to compensate for noise, fumes and lifting is simply another way of accepting health and safety hazards. In Chapter 3 it was suggested that one of the main objectives of method study should be to remove hazards and poor working conditons.

Union representatives should also be wary of the inbuilt **sexism** of most allowance tables. There may be some case for women's personal needs allowance to be greater than that normally given for men but, for the sake of unity, the anomaly should be scrapped and the higher figure given to men as well as women. There is no point in getting involved in detailed arguments with employers and consultants on this issue; it should be clarified before any studies are carried out or, at the latest, before any standard times are issued. It is perfectly rational, reasonable and respectable to respond to the employer's objections by pointing out that the matter is shop/plant/union policy.

In some public sector incentive schemes, the issue was resolved by setting a unisex allowance for personal needs and fatigue at 10%. This seemed like a sensible compromise between the 9% and 11% in the ILO tables, until it was realised that in many cases the majority of the workers covered by the scheme were women! There may be no further need to expose the empty claims of work study practitioners to a scientific basis for their profession. However, it is difficult to resist pointing out that the table reproduced on pages 57–58 suggests that men and women are equally affected by noise, yet physical monotony is less damaging to women. This kind of nonsense should be buried alongside the attitudes responsible for it.

Allowances and machine elements

It was stated above that relaxation allowances should be added to all elements in the work cycle and that this is usually the case in practice. However, I know of at least three cases where allowances were not allocated to machine-controlled elements. In one of them this sleight of hand was not discovered until some three years after the incentive scheme began. The omission was justified by the employer on the ground that while the machine was working the operative could rest! Hopefully it will not be necessary to argue this one but, if it is, workers can point out that a person operating a machine is still subject to environmental pressures and conditions, will still experience 'basic fatigue' and will still be responsible for the correct functioning of the machine.

Standard times

Once the agreed allowances have been added to all repetitive and occasional elements in the work cycle, the standard time can be calculated and submitted to union representatives for approval. At this stage the standard time might be called a **'standard minute value'** (SMV) or a **'work value'** (WV). Once agreed, it becomes the time in which an average qualified worker will be expected to carry out that task continually over an eight-hour day. If the worker achieves this consistently, then he or she is said to be working at **standard performance**. Figures 17 and 18, which continue with the milling example used earlier, show how the standard time would be totted-up under varying degrees of union influence.

Figure 17: *Adding allowances and calculating the standard time for the task or work cycle*

Element	Basic time	Allowance	Standard time
Repetitive element A	.16	20%	.19
Repetitive element B	.81	20%	.97
Repetitive element C	.20	20%	.24
Repetitive element D	.10	20%	.12
Repetitive element E	.31	20%	.37
Repetitive element F	.12	20%	.14
		Total =	**2.03 standard mins**
Occasional element 1	.03	20%	.04
Occasional element 2	.04	20%	.05
Occasional element 3	.12	20%	.14
		Total =	**.23 standard mins**
Contingency allowance at 5%			
($\frac{5}{100} \times 2.03$ mins)		=	**.10 standard mins**
standard minute value		=	**2.36 standard mins**

Assuming that the standard minute value for the milling operation, as calculated in Figure 17, was arrived at after trade-union negotiations on such issues as the method of work, ratings, the allocation of occasional elements, contingencies, ineffective time and allowances, a comparison can be made with the more usual case where the employer has a free hand. Leaving aside ratings, it would not be outrageous, on the basis of some of the studies I have seen, to suggest that the employer might well make the following decisions:

a) element B is machine-controlled – rate at 75 and give no allowances;

b) disregard or overlook the last two occasional elements due to short studies or the absence of an effective trade-union challenge;

c) contingency allowance at 2% as 'company policy'; and

d) relaxation allowances at 11% (9% for fatigue and personal needs and 2% for standing).

The effect of these decisions is shown in Figure 18.

Figure 18: *Standard minute value (amended)*

Element	Basic time	Allowance	Standard time
Repetitive element A	.16	11%	.18
Repetitive element B*	.61	nil	.61
Repetitive element C	.20	11%	.22
Repetitive element D	.10	11%	.11
Repetitive element E	.35	11%	.39
Repetitive element F	.12	11%	.13
		Total =	**1.64 standard mins**
Occasional element 3	.12	11%	.13
		Total =	**.13 standard mins**

Contingency allowance at 2%

$(\frac{2}{100} \times 1.64 \text{ mins})$ =   **.03 standard mins**

standard minute value   =   **1.80 standard mins**

*Element B, which is machine-controlled, has been reduced because it has been rated at 75, $(.81 \times \frac{75}{100} = .61$ basic minutes).

The examples in Figures 17 and 18 are not intended to show 'right' from 'wrong' or even 'good' from 'bad'; they simply demonstrate that standard times produced through time study are negotiable. Remember that, to achieve **standard performance** over the day, the worker has to consistently perform the task in the time set by the standard minute value. Clearly, negotiations on the standard minute value itself will affect output, productivity, pay and jobs. To show this more clearly, the effects of the two different standard minute values on output are shown in Figure 19.

Figure 19: *Effects upon output of two different standard minute values*

	A (Fig. 17)	B (Fig. 18)
Standard minute value for milling a casting:	2.36 sms	1.80 sms
Output in continuous 8 hours work:	$\frac{480 \text{ mins}}{2.36}$	$\frac{480 \text{ mins}}{1.80}$
=	203 castings	267 castings

The worker unfortunate enough to be working to the standard minute value in 'B' has to produce 64 extra castings (31% more) than the worker in 'A' – yet both are working at **standard performance**! Or, to put it another way, the output which plant 'A' produces with 20 workers can be produced in plant 'B' with 15. Can this really happen in practice? Doesn't this mean that 'scientific management' is a fraud? As trade unionists, we really should not be surprised; most of us can point to other organisations where workers doing the same job earn more/less pay, get longer/shorter holidays or have produce less/more to satisfy their employer. The reasons for the variations can usually be traced back to the level of trade-union organisation. Work study does not **neutralise** the balance of power between worker and employer, it **reinforces** the employer.

Policy allowances

A policy allowance is intolerable to some consultants. Quite simply it is an extra percentage allowance stuck on top of the standard minute value. The aim is deliberately to inflate the standard time so that workers reach higher performance levels and therefore higher bonus earnings. Employers may be persuaded to concede policy allowances where a standard time-based incentive scheme replaces an old piecework scheme, and the new scheme yields lower bonus earnings than the old one. Policy allowances may also be applied where employers are seeking workers' co-operation to overcome temporary production difficulties which adversely affect bonus earnings.

Where an old bonus scheme is being replaced by a new one, employers often attempt to bring about a long-term wage cut by proposing that only existing employees should receive the policy allowances. The effect is to turn new workers into cheaper labour by demanding that they produce more for the same earnings.

Policy allowances make nonsense of any notions of 'purity', 'accuracy' and 'objectivity' which might still be attached to work study.

Summary of Chapter 5

■ **Allowances** are added to the basic time for each repetitive and occasional element to produce a standard time for each element.

■ The **contingency allowance** is supposed to cover all minor delays and incidents and is usually calculated as a percentage of the total standard minutes for all repetitive elements in the work cycle.

■ The **total standard minutes** for repetitive elements, occasional elements and the contingency allowance are added together to produce the standard time for the task or work cycle.

■ The standard time might be called a **standard minute value** (SMV) or a **work value** (WV).

■ Allowances may be allocated in two parts; the **constant** allowance and the **variable** allowance.

■ Allowances are **negotiable**.

■ Employers may attempt to apply allowances differently between **men** and **women**.

■ Employers may attempt to **avoid** allocating allowances to some elements, particularly those which are machine-controlled.

■ A **policy allowance** may be negotiated to protect current earnings.

Checklist on allowances and standard times

■ Does your agreement state that allowances are subject to **negotiation**?

■ Will allowances be allocated to **all** elements?

■ Have you considered a **fixed allowance** to be applied across the shop/department/plant?

■ Have you considered setting up a **stewards' committee** especially to examine the allowances?

■ Do you **understand** the system of allocating allowances which your employer is proposing?

■ Do you think about allowances as **'rest time'**? (Remember, a 10% allowance is 10% of your work time which, over eight hours is 48 minutes; 20% is 1 hour 36 minutes rest.)

■ Does your agreement require that the final standard time and accompanying calculations be submitted to union representatives for **approval**?

■ Do union representatives have sufficient time and facilities to **discuss** the standard minute value with the members concerned?

■ Does your agreement state that the standard minute value can only be **amended** with the approval of the membership?

■ Are **policy allowances** appropriate? If so, will they apply to all members, present and future?

■ Have you compared the output levels required to reach **standard** performance with the **normal average** levels?

6.
Pre-determined motion time systems (PMTS)

Methods time measurement / other PMT systems / humans or machines?

PMTS has been used extensively in engineering, printing, the National Health Service and in office work. Its users claim that it is much more acceptable to workers because it does not use the stopwatch or rating. In fact, this suggestion is completely untrue – a piece of crude deception dreamed up to overcome workers' opposition to work study. The AUEW once called it the 'cardboard stopwatch'.

The system is based upon the theory that, within practical limits, the time required for all experts to perform a fundamental action is constant. Work study practitioners have discovered that workers all over the world are **human beings** whose arms, hands and fingers move in a pattern determined by the way in which human bodies are constructed. After this discovery it was logical for 'scientific management' to suggest that time study had not gone far enough by merely breaking jobs down into tasks and elements. The creative brilliance of modern management revealed that all task elements consist of a range of body movements by the worker. As there was a limit to the range of body movements required (if necessary, they could be limited by management), each motion could be coded and given a set time – a **predetermined time**.

All the study engineer has to do is list all the body movements necessary to perform an element, read off the times for each movement from a prepared table and add them up to produce a time for the element. No rating and no stopwatch it seems.

Methods time measurement

One of the most widely-used PMT systems is methods time measurement (MTM). MTM-1 consists of a number of tables which list some 15 body movements, called 'basic motions', among them 'reach', 'grasp', 'move', 'eye focus' and so on. Each basic motion is further classified with a number of variables such as, distance reached, weight moved and degree of difficulty involved. In total, around 500 basic motions are listed in the MTM-1 tables, each with a predetermined time.

As one would expect, these basic motions are performed too rapidly for even the most zealous work study practitioner to record in minutes and seconds. For this reason, a new way of measuring time was developed called a **'time measurement unit'** (tmu). One tmu is equivalent to .00001 of an hour, that is, one hundred-thousandth of an hour. As there are 3,600 seconds in an hour, we can divide 100,000 by 3,600 to find that there are 27.8 tmus in one second! Not content with even this level of 'scientific' accuracy, the MTM-1 tables also give times in *tenths* of a tmu.

Figure 20: *Example of times given on MTM-1 tables*

Basic motion	code	time
Reach for spanner, 10 centimetres, hanging on hook	R 10 A	6.1 tmus
Move object weighing half a kilogram, 20 centimetres to an exact location	M 20 C	11.7 tmus

If you are quick with figures you may have calculated that 6.1 tmus are just over one-fifth of a second and 11.7 tmus, just over two-fifths of a second. As one can imagine, the amount of paperwork involved in analysing the basic motions in all the elements which constitute a task is enormous. For this reason, MTM-1 has been rather expensive to apply and has normally been confined to highly repetitive, short-cycle work (although this has not prevented it from being used in National Health Service schemes). Clearly, there is a vast amount of detail to be learned by MTM-1 users and they are expected to attend an intensive training course before being let loose on the world. To attempt to cover the content of that course would be both futile and sickening.

Apart from offering an alternative to direct time study, MTM-1 provides employers with the opportunity to **'visualise'** tasks being performed without actually having to observe them. Work stations, benches and methods of work can be designed before any workers are hired. MTM data can be fed into a computer along with the basic motions considered to be necessary, and the computer will deliver the best sequence, allocate the movements to right and left hands and calculate the job time in tmus.

A full-time union officer once told me that on visiting a new plant for negotiations on pay and conditions, he was informed by management that work methods, job times and production targets had already been calculated using MTM – this before a single worker had been taken on!

Unions in the USA have vigorously attacked most PMT systems and the AFL/CIO (the US equivalent of the TUC), commenced its advice to trade unions facing the use of PMTS with the following two lines:

1 Resist and oppose their introduction.
2 Eliminate them where they exist.

This advice comes from the country where PMTS was invented, developed and first tried on workers on a large scale. In Britain, the AUEW has attacked MTM users for making ridiculous claims about its 'objectivity', although one would hardly expect techniques for increasing managerial control to be 'objective'.

The MTM tables were compiled after thousands of hours of studying cine film of workers carrying out a whole range of operations. Sophisticated timing methods were used and the workers were rated for skill and efficiency. The end result of this work is the MTM tables which their users claim **eliminate** rating and the stopwatch! It is true that modern work study practitioners who use MTM (or other PMT systems) do not have to rely on the stopwatch and are not required to make rating assessments. This is because stopwatch timings and rating assessments are built into the MTM tables. There are a few issues that ought to be mentioned in comparing MTM times with the standard times produced by conventional time study, and these are covered below.

The stopwatch

Not used when actually applying MTM except to time machine speeds and machine-controlled elements.

Rating

Not overtly used; all MTM times have a built-in rating assessment of 83 on the BSI 0–100 scale. Employers usually adjust the MTM time by multiplying by 83 and dividing by 100 to produce the equivalent of a basic time.

Allowances

No allowances for fatigue, personal needs and working conditions are included in MTM times; they are still a matter for negotiation.

Other PMT systems

A number of PMT systems have been developed, based upon MTM-1. Some of these are called **'second generation'** systems because they combine basic motions to make up a single operation or element. For example, the basic motions 'reach' and 'grasp' are combined to produce 'get'. These combined motions are sometimes further combined to produce whole elements and tasks. These 'second, third and fourth generation' systems are very popular with employers because they are relatively cheap to apply, cannot be understood readily by the workforce and are littered with mumbo-jumbo which passes for 'science'. Sometimes, the element times are worked out in one plant and applied at another, with no regard for variations in working conditions or layout. Much of the data used in the NHS schemes was compiled in just one, quite modern, hospital. A brief description of some PMT systems in use is given in Appendix 1 at the end of this book.

Humans or machines?

Amongst the problems for union representatives faced with PMTS, is the fact that study sheets or computer readouts are extremely complex to deal with, unless indoctrination (called 'training') has been given. This is one of its advantages to employers. The United Automobile Workers of the USA have consistently attacked PMTS as being highly subjective and unscientific. This has led them to centre their attack on the theory underlying PMTS – that the time for all fundamental motions is a constant. The UAW has enlisted a great deal of academic support to point out that the time taken for one basic motion will depend upon the motions preceding and following it.

This approach is basically flawed in that it does not attack the system but simply criticises the data tables. It is virtually asking PMTS practitioners to calculate adjustment factors for variations caused by the immediate circumstances under which each body motion is made, which would only complicate the issue further. Nearer the point is the view of Dr Pearce Davis of the Illinois Technical Institute, quoted in the UAW paper on work standards:

> Such industrial engineering procedures as MTM are not pure science; they are at best 'scientific art'. The exercise of human judgement in all methods of standards setting is inevitable and inherent. Nor is it likely to be otherwise because of the nature of the procedures themselves. In addition to the continuing presence of human judgement, there is always the further problem of the degree of variation in the exercise of human judgement. This degree of variation depends fundamentally upon one's philosophy of life, on an individual's general attitudes towards the goals of management, or an individual's level of impartiality, and upon numerous other similar conditioning factors.

This is a somewhat long-winded way of saying something that all trade unionists are aware of – 'fairness' depends upon whose side you are on. Work study practitioners see human beings as units of energy, hands separate from brains; those who do not will eventually crack up when the disgusting and dehumanising nature of their profession sinks in. The continual search for the 'best' method leads not to the method which is most fulfilling to the worker concerned, nor to the method which enables the worker to derive satisfaction from what he or she is doing, nor even to the method which is the sanest or safest. Under modern production methods, workers are expected to support an army of production engineers, production planners, co-ordinators, instructors and progress chasers. Can this really be the most 'efficient' use of human resources? Nevertheless, 'scientific management' continues to serve the interests of employers whose aim in modern industrial societies is to take the study of human labour to the level of machine design.

Part Two

Incentive schemes

Introduction to Part Two

Part Two looks at how standard times are used to assess the performance of a worker or group of workers and how performance figures can be used to determine pay. While the introduction of incentive schemes can make it even more difficult to maintain stable earnings, the tendency to concentrate too heavily of their financial aspects can damage trade-union organisation and control. For this reason, Chapter 6 discusses threats to organisation and solidarity which are often unforeseen or overlooked.

It is worth stating again that, at the point where a new incentive scheme based upon standard times is to be installed, the employer has already gained a number of advantages. Apart from consultants' fees and the wages and facilities for the study engineers, most of these gains will have cost next to nothing by way of wages to employees. As a result of employee co-operation with work study, the employer will have secured all or most of the following:

a) a thorough knowledge of work organisation, skills, customs and practices, demarcations, unofficial activities and effort levels;

b) revised workplace layouts, new patterns of work, the introduction of new equipment and machinery and new procedures for planning, recording and controlling output;

c) new methods of work, specified in detail, a re-allocation of responsibilities and duties between workers, and new staffing levels;

d) standard times for all jobs; and

e) solid, reliable information with which to plan long-term changes and investment.

Of course, the degree of change achieved at this stage will depend upon the depth of the investigation, the resources committed and the co-operation of the employees. Where a thorough investigation involving detailed method studies has been undertaken, employers will have made significant increases in productivity and strengthened their control over the organisation. The productivity improvements will have been made possible through reduced delays, reduced waste, increased production time, and elimination of restrictive customs and practices and, possibly, reduced staffing.

The employer now has everything necessary to reduce costs and, in the private sector, to increase profits – except the continued co-operation of the workers; this is where the **bonus scheme** comes in. If workers are to be encouraged to comply with the new methods *and* to raise their pace of work, extra money usually has to appear on the negotiating table. Isn't this where the employer starts to pay? If so, where does this extra money come from?

In reality, workers always pay for their own bonus earnings. The pool of money which will finance the increased earnings can come from two sources. Firstly, the workers increase their output to earn a bonus, which means that the employer does not have to take on extra labour or offer overtime to achieve the same result. In this case the bonus earnings are financed through overtime earnings *not* paid and labour *not* hired. Secondly, the increased output is either not needed or cannot be sold, in which case the number of workers is reduced and the wages which would have been paid will finance the bonus scheme for those who remain.

There is nothing particularly miraculous or subtle about this. Work study and incentive schemes do not, of themselves, **generate** money; they indicate ways and means of saving and distributing it. The work study-based incentive schemes introduced into hospitals, schools and local authority services make this abundantly clear. These employers have no intention of increasing output in the form of more and better services to the community. It is a condition of public services schemes that they are self-financing and many local authority stewards are familiar with agreements which detail methods, tasks, standard times and bonuses and then go on to state (to quote one example) that, 'the number of employees required will be reduced from 20 to 15 through natural wastage and a freeze on recruitment.' It is obvious that where there is a limited amount of work to go round, the effect of each worker raising output is to reduce the number of workers required, *unless* there is a simultaneous and compensatory reduction in normal working hours.

In most work study-based incentive schemes, workers find that the focus of attention is standard performance. Management talk about it, consultants suggest that it is easy to achieve, bonus targets hinge upon it and, eventually, the membership will refer to it as though it was an invention of their own. The British Standards Institution definition of standard performance (BS 51004) states:

> Standard performance is the rate of output which qualified workers
> will naturally achieve over the working day or shift, provided that
> they know and adhere to the specified method and provided that
> they are motivated to apply themselves to their work.

The **'motivation'**, of course, is the extra money earned through the incentive scheme and this works in two ways. When a scheme is first introduced, bonus earnings are seen by the workers as an 'extra' and something to strive for. Once the scheme has been in operation for some time and the workers have become accustomed to their new level of earnings, standard performance becomes the norm and any drop below that level may well appear as a **wage cut**.

This is the attraction of some incentive schemes to employers: they provide an automatic regulator on wage costs. If the workload drops, labour costs are reduced as bonus earnings decline. Standard performance will always represent a significant increase in output per worker when compared with the levels prior to work study (see again Figure 2). This increase is often obscured by the use of the word 'standard' which has a comfortable, neutral ring. It seems to imply 'par for the course' or even 'normal' yet, as we have seen in the time study chapters, standard performance is measured by using standard times which are subject to opinion and negotiation.

7.
Performance and measured work

In a large plant, bonus schemes will usually be introduced department by department and an agreement will be negotiated for each department laying out the specific terms and conditions of the scheme. This departmental agreement may be called the **'work specification part two'**. Part one of the work specification, which usually covers the general terms relating to the use of work study and the introduction of incentive schemes, will apply to everybody. Part two details work practices, duties and staffing, and contains a table of standard minute values (SMVs) for most of the tasks normally carried out within the department. It will also state how work is to be recorded and how bonus is to be calculated.

For a worker to achieve standard performance over an eight-hour day (480 minutes), the standard minute values for the tasks performed throughout the day must total 480 standard minutes. Therefore, standard performance is 60 standard minutes of work in each hour. If we refer back to our engineering friend working the milling machine (Figure 17), we can see how this works in practice. The SMV for milling a casting was 2.36 standard minutes; if he produced 203 castings in eight hours he will have achieved standard performance (203 castings × 2.36 standard minutes per casting = 479.08 standard minutes).

Most schemes will operate what is called a **'performance index'** (PI), on which standard performance is given a figure of 100, just as it is on the BSI 0–100 rating scale. The purpose of the performance index is to compare each worker's performance in relation to standard. Obviously, workers will not perform at standard day in and day out so the performance index is one way of assessing how far below or above standard each worker's performance happens to be. The most common performance index starts at 75 and goes on to a cut-off point, or ceiling, somewhere above 100.

In standard time-based incentive schemes, the performance index is used to work out bonus earnings. Standard (100) will pay an agreed level of bonus for each hour worked; 90 will pay so much less and 110 so much more. The beginning and end of the performance index, and the amount of bonus paid at each level, are entirely matters for negotiation.

Calculating a worker's performance is relatively simple. First of all the worker has to book all the tasks which he or she has carried out during the day; the number of tasks is then multiplied by the SMV for each task to give a total number of standard minutes earned during the day. The following formula is then used to calculate the worker's performance:

$$\frac{\text{Total standard minutes earned during day} \times 100}{\text{Total actual minutes spent working}} = \text{Performance}$$

Using this formula, the work study office can calculate the performance achieved even though actual output may vary from day to day. Figure 21 shows a couple of examples.

Figure 21: *Calculating performance*

---

1 Output: 186 castings
   SMV: 2.36 standard minutes
   Working time: 8 hours (480 minutes)
                    $186 \times 2.36 = 438.96$ sms
                    $\dfrac{438.96 \times 100}{480 \text{ minutes}} = 91$ performance (91.3)

2 Output: 186 castings
   SMV: 2.36 standard minutes
   Working time: 7 hours (420 minutes)
                    $186 \times 2.36 = 438.96$ sms
                    $\dfrac{438.96 \times 100}{420 \text{ minutes}} = 105$ performance (104.5)

In practice, workers will probably carry out a range of different tasks in each day and each task will be given its own separate SMV. This may include an SMV for end-of-shift cleaning as well as an SMV for various clerical tasks, such as completing time sheets and booking work.

Workers on continuous or lengthy production runs will find that SMVs are issued for a stated quantity of work. For example, workers packing cans into boxes on the end of a production line may be issued with an SMV of, say, 25 sms per 100 boxes packed. A chemical worker mixing solvents may be given an SMV of 40 sms per 50-gallon batch. Printers may find that their performances are mainly calculated on the basis of copies printed, say, an SMV of 5 sms per 1000 sheets.

Through the process of studying, rating, timing and negotiation, each worker will have been issued with a standard minute value for almost all aspects of their daily work. This system of calculating performances also enables the performances of workers on totally different kinds of work to be directly compared (see Figure 22).

Figure 22: *Calculating and comparing performances*

Example A: Printer

Work booked	*Quantity*	*SMV*	*Total sms*
Prepare print run	1	20 sms	20
Print (sheets)	60,000	5 sms per 1,000	300
Load paper to machine	12	10 sms	120
End-of-shift cleaning	1	20 sms	20
		Total =	**460 sms**

Time spent = 8 hours

Performance $= \dfrac{460 \text{ sms}}{480 \text{ mins}} \times 100 = \textbf{96}$

Example B: Engineer

Work booked	*Quantity*	*SMV*	*Total sms*
Mill castings type A1	150	2.36 sms	354
Mill castings type B2	30	4.5 sms	135
End-of-shift cleaning	1	8 sms	8
		Total =	**497 sms**

Time spent = 7½ hours

Performance $= \dfrac{497 \text{ sms}}{450 \text{ mins}} \times 100 = \textbf{110}$

Once performances have been calculated, usually over a week, the bonus earnings for an individual or a group of workers can be read off from a table which shows the agreed amount of bonus per hour for each level of performance. Once the SMV for each task is set it then applies to all workers carrying out that task. Some workers will achieve higher performances than others simply by building up more standard minutes over the day through producing more output. In this sense every worker has an output whether it is sheets printed, castings milled, letters typed, hospital wards cleaned or pints of blood collected. (Yes, even the blood donor service has an incentive scheme!)

Those unfamiliar with work study incentives may find the concept of 'earning' standard minutes a bit strange. It's sometimes useful to think of standard minutes as points. If a worker wants to achieve standard performance over an hour, then the total points for all the work done in that hour must add up to 60. If cleaning a normal window for example, is worth 5 points, then 12 windows will have to be cleaned to make 60 points, i.e. standard. Smaller windows may be worth 4 points and larger ones worth 6 or 7. Points or standard minutes, it's the same thing.

In the two examples in Figure 22, both workers have had a relatively uncomplicated day. Each item of work had been given a standard minute value and they had been fully occupied on **'measured work'**. (Measured work is all work for which a standard minute value has been agreed.) Of course, this will not always be the case; other activities or interruptions are bound to occur which have no set standard minute value. Generally speaking, these other activities can be covered under two headings:

a) waiting time; and b) unmeasured work.

Waiting time, sometimes called 'lost time', is relatively straightforward. It covers all time spent not working while waiting for work, instructions, materials, repairs to a machine – in fact, anything which can be classified as a delay.

Unmeasured work is work which has no standard minute value. It may have been left unmeasured either because the study engineer has not yet got round to studying it, or because it is difficult to measure. Unmeasured work may also cover experimenting with new jobs, new methods of work, or new machines and materials.

These two categories of what management would call 'unproductive work' are major sources of instability in earnings, of disputes and of general frustration. There is no established way of dealing with them, simply good practice and bad practice; what you get in the end depends entirely upon negotiation. The effects on pay of waiting time and unmeasured work, and some of the negotiating issues involved, are discussed in the next chapter.

8.
Waiting time and unmeasured work

Where work study-based incentives are introduced for the first time, it is a common employers' tactic to suggest that the bonus is actually based upon **effort** and not **output**. To demonstrate this, they point out that standard times have been set for all sorts of non-productive work such as cleaning, setting up, work booking and so on: bonus can be earned even though the worker is not actually producing. This is usually the foundation for a major negotiating trap. If work study has been scrupulously applied, then it may well be true that standard times will have been set for all incidental preparatory work and the usual bits and pieces which occur in most jobs. Although important, they may not amount to much when taken over a full week compared with the time spent actually producing. The next step for the employer is to point out that, as bonus earnings are determined by effort, the logic is: 'constant effort – constant bonus' and 'no effort – no bonus'.

If this line of reasoning is accepted, it means two things. Firstly, productivity can be increased by changing methods of work without increasing earnings. Secondly, as waiting time involves no effort, it should be paid at nil bonus. Employers have not been terribly successful with the first argument. Few organised workers will accept that the introduction of new equipment requiring no extra effort on the part of the worker permits management to slash the agreed standard times and pay the same bonus for much greater output.

However, they have been quite successful with the second argument and a great proportion of work study-based incentives actually do pay nil bonus for waiting time, irrespective of its cause. This issue causes much aggravation in the long term, especially when waiting time is caused by management incompetence or inefficiency.

To understand what happens in practice, it is necessary to explain the way in which bonus tables are used in relation to the performance achieved. Among the trade unions which have policies on bonus schemes, some suggest that bonus earnings should be **'straight proportional'** or better. Straight proportional simply means that earnings should rise in direct proportion to the rise in output. When plotted on a graph, a straight proportional scheme shows as a straight line. This will be dealt with in more detail later but, to understand how waiting time affects bonus earnings, it is enough to say that a straight proportional scheme usually fits the framework shown in Figure 23.

Figure 23: *Bonus payments in a straight proportional scheme*

Performance	Earnings
75 ('normal')	Basic rate plus nil bonus
100 ('standard')	Basic rate plus 33.3%
125 ('ceiling')	Basic rate plus 66.6%

If you look back to the rating tables in Figure 11, you can see that the performance figures of 75, 100 and 125 are described (in rating terms) by reference to different speeds of walking. Standard performance (100) is said to involve a one-third increase in effort over normal performance (75), therefore a bonus of 33.3% of the basic rate is the usual payment. The ceiling performance (125) is said to involve a 66.6% increase in effort and therefore attracts a bonus of 66.6% of the basic rate. What this means in practice is that a performance of 75 is equal to the fall-back rate, or basic rate, and no bonus is paid. Since an incentive scheme cannot pay less than nil bonus employers will suggest that all waiting time should be paid at a performance level of 75. In effect, this means that the workers finance their own waiting time out of the bonus they have already built up on measured work. This is achieved by averaging out the various levels of performance over the week, as shown in Figure 24.

Figure 24: *Averaging performances over a week*

Working time: 40 hours
Measured work: 35 hours
Waiting time: 5 hours

Standard minutes earned on measured work: 2100 sms

Measured work performance $= \dfrac{2100 \text{ sms} \times 100}{35 \text{ hours} \times 60 \text{ mins}}$

$= 100$ performance

Average performance over the week
Measured work: 35 hours at 100 $= 3500$
Waiting time: 5 hours at 75 $= 375$
Total performance credits $= 3875$
Average performance $= \dfrac{3875}{40 \text{ hours}}$ $= 96.8 \ (97)$

Although standard (100) was achieved when measured work was available, the performance has been reduced overall to 97 because of the claw-back effect of waiting time paid at 75.

The agreement covering the payment of waiting time and unmeasured work is absolutely crucial to the future stability of earnings. While employers will propose nil bonus for waiting time, they cannot use the 'no effort – no bonus' argument for unmeasured work because effort is clearly involved. Invariably some performance figure between 75 and 100 is proposed for unmeasured work (usually nearer 75). The whole 'effort' argument is insidious and trade unionists should avoid trying to counter it or use it. The simplest negotiating line to adopt (though not the easiest to achieve) is to argue that members should not suffer a drop in earnings or earnings opportunity because of factors beyond their control. In effect, this would mean demanding that waiting time and unmeasured work should be paid at **average performance** – usually the worker's average performance when engaged on measured work.

As you would expect, a wide range of agreements has been negotiated to cover these two issues. The worst I have seen pays waiting time at 75 performance and unmeasured work at 80. The code of requirements for National Health Service schemes pays waiting time at 75, some unmeasured work at 75 and other types of unmeasured work at the operative's average measured work performance. Compromise agreements to be found in other industries include some where the first two hours of waiting time per week are paid at 75, with any further waiting time paid at average performance.

The best schemes, in terms of maintaining stable earnings, are those where all non-measured activities, including waiting time, are paid at average performance. Figure 25 illustrates the effect on earnings of the best and worst agreements on waiting time and unmeasured work.

Figure 25: *Comparison of agreements on waiting time and unmeasured work*

Basic information

Working week:	40 hours
Measured work (MW):	30 hours at 105 performance
Waiting time (WT):	6 hours
Unmeasured work (UW):	4 hours

Agreement A	*Agreement B*
WT paid at 75	WT paid at MW performance
UW paid at 80	UW paid at MW performance
MW = 30 hrs × 105 = 3150	MW = 30 hrs × 105 = 3150
WT = 6 hrs × 75 = 450	WT = 6 hrs × 105 = 630
UW = 4 hrs × 80 = 320	UW = 4 hrs × 105 = 420
Total credits = **3920**	Total credits = **4200**
Weekly performance = $\dfrac{3920}{40 \text{ hrs}}$ = 98	Weekly performance = $\dfrac{4200}{40 \text{ hrs}}$ = 105

Figure 24 shows that there could be a seven-point difference brought about entirely by the terms of the agreements negotiated. The benefits of a good agreement escalate as waiting time increases as a proportion of normal working time. The gap could be much greater than that shown in the example. On a straight proportional scheme, the bonus percentage to be paid for 98 and 105 performances can be worked out by calculating the percentage increase above normal (75) as follows:

A   98 performance $= \dfrac{(98-75) \times 100}{75} = 30.7\%$

B   105 performance $= \dfrac{(105-75) \times 100}{75} = 40\%$

If we assume a basic rate of £2.00 per hour, the performance under agreement A would pay a bonus of 61.4 pence per hour (30.7% of £2.00), while the performance under agreement B would provide 80 pence per hour (40% of £2.00) – a difference of £7.44 over the week for the identical amount of work! All the careful work which union representatives may have put in to achieve reasonable standard times can be lost in bad agreements covering the operation of the incentive scheme.

These issues need to be fully explained to the membership and should be pressed at an early stage in negotiations – certainly before the employer has the benefit of method studies and method changes tucked away. The issue of waiting time clearly shows one of the major benefits of incentive schemes for employers, namely the opportunity to cut earnings when work is slack or to deliberately contrive a shortage of work with the same effect.

9.
The connection between performance and pay

The amount of bonus paid for the level of performance achieved is entirely a matter for negotiation. The best scheme is probably one which consolidates all bonus earnings into the basic rate, but this defeats the entire object as far as management is concerned, and they will not be keen to sign on the dotted line. Nevertheless, it can remain as a long-term trade-union objective and we will return to the issue in a later chapter.

In all performance-related incentive schemes, where the intention is to allow bonus earnings to fluctuate, bonus starts to be earned at a point on the performance index some way below standard (100), and stops at some agreed point above standard – usually called the **ceiling**. The way in which bonus payments increase between the starting point and the ceiling is referred to as the **'bonus line'**, or **'bonus curve'**. One type, the 'straight proportional', has already been discussed. Probably the most common, being used in all public service schemes, it has all the appearance of being 'fair and reasonable' and is the minimum which some trade unions will accept. For these reasons it makes a useful reference with which to compare any scheme, particularly some of the more complex types which consultants and employers sometimes propose. Drawn on a graph, it is immediately obvious that bonus earnings rise in a straight line in direct proportion to the increase in performance (see Figure 26). However, *not* every scheme which shows on a graph as a straight line is straight proportional, as will be illustrated later.

Straight proportional schemes have their origin in old-fashioned piecework where labour costs were controlled by setting a price per piece produced. The higher the individual's output, the higher his or her gross earnings, with the price per piece (which is another way of saying unit labour costs) remaining constant.

Figure 26: *A conventional straight proportional bonus scheme*

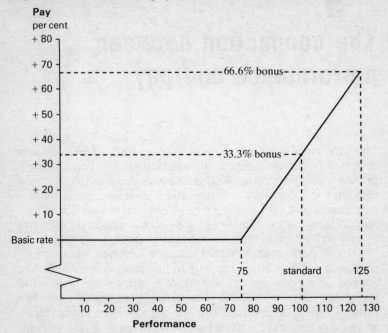

Basic rate is paid for all performances at 75 and below; above 75 the bonus earned rises in direct relation to the increase in performance until the cut-off or ceiling is reached.

Labour costs per unit of output are usually calculated by dividing a week's wages by the output produced in that week. Figure 27 shows the connection between piecework, the straight proportional scheme and performance based upon standard times.

The example in Figure 27 shows that, in the case of piece-work, **unit labour costs** remain **constant** because the price per piece is constant; there is a direct relationship between output and pay. However, in performance-based schemes the relationship is not quite so direct. Although the SMV remains constant, the workers on this type of scheme are not paid in relation to the number of **standard minutes** they accumulate but in accordance with their **performance**. The example in Figure 27 also shows that in straight proportional schemes the relationship is pretty much

Figure 27: *Output, performance and pay in a) a piecework scheme, and b) a straight proportional bonus scheme*

	1	2	3
A	normal $\longrightarrow$ plus 33.3%		$\longrightarrow$ plus 66.6%

	1	2	3
a) Hourly output:	9 units	12 units	15 units
b) 40 hour output:	360 units	480 units	600 units
c) Price per unit:	constant at 20p per unit		
d) Pay:	£72.00	£96.00	£120.00
e) Unit labour costs: d) ÷ b)	£ .20	£ .20	£ .20

B *In a bonus scheme based upon standard minutes and performance, the figures would come out the same but would be presented as follows:*

	1	2	3
a) Hourly output:	9 units	12 units	15 units
b) 40 hour output:	360 units	480 units	600 units
c) Standard minute value:	constant at 5 sms per unit		
d) Performance:	75	100	125
e) Basic pay:	£72.00	£72.00	£ 72.00
f) Bonus:	nil	£24.00	£ 48.00
g) Gross pay:	£72.00	£96.00	£120.00
h) Unit labour costs: g) ÷ b)	£ .20	£ .20	£ .20

In this example, performance has been calculated using the formula shown on page 77.

the same as that in piecework, but not all schemes are like that.

Not all schemes provide a third increase in pay for a third increase in output, let alone a two-thirds increase in pay for a similar increase in output. In some schemes, bonus earnings rise at a slower rate than output so that as performance goes *up*, unit labour costs come *down*; these schemes are called **regressive** which is a polite consultant's term for daylight robbery. There can be no justification in trade-union terms for any scheme which permits employers to pay a lower price per unit as performance or output increases.

Labour is not the only cost involved in production and while employers can afford to pay higher wages for higher output, they do not have to pay higher rent, higher rates, higher insurance, higher interest and so on, as a *direct consequence* of output being increased. By and large, these costs remain fairly constant whatever level of output is achieved. However, as a percentage of total unit costs these 'overhead' costs actually *decline* as output rises, thereby reducing the cost per unit.

Of course employers will argue that their rents, rates, etc. *are* rising, although not as a consequence of higher output; but this is true for workers as well. As a general economic argument the cost of living issue may be well worth pursuing. As an excuse to rob workers by fraud, it is a red herring.

It is often overlooked that, even in straight proportional schemes, employers can make substantial savings through an overall reduction in unit costs – a saving which rarely appears on the negotiating table. If a group of workers is persuaded to increase output by, say, one-third and the employer is prepared to increase pay by one-third, the extra costs required to finance the increased output are virtually limited to the extra pay to the workers directly concerned. Of course, the overall costs of materials rise, but not the cost of material in each unit produced. On the other hand, in addition to the costs associated with rents, rates, insurance and loan interest, there are many other costs which also remain constant even though output rises, such as wages to 'nonproductive' or indirect staff, canteen costs, depreciation, lighting and heating. Figure 28 gives a general example.

Figure 28: *Labour and overhead costs in a straight proportional scheme*

Weekly output	Direct wage costs	Overhead costs	Total operating costs	Unit costs
480 units	£ 72.00	£150.00	£222.00	£0.46
640 units	£ 96.00	£150.00	£246.00	£0.38
800 units	£120.00	£150.00	£270.00	£0.34

There are schemes which attempt to share some of the savings on overhead costs made as a result of increased output. This is done by allowing bonus earnings to increase *faster* than output; these schemes are usually called **progressive**. Figure 29 shows how regressive and progressive schemes compare with straight-proportional when shown on a graph. Although all three produce a straight line on the graph paper, only the straight-proportional pays a bonus of 33.3% at standard performance. The regressive in the example pays 25%, although it could pay even lower percentages than that. The progressive pays a bonus of 50% of the basic rate at standard performance.

Figure 29: *Regressive, progressive and straight proportional bonus schemes compared*

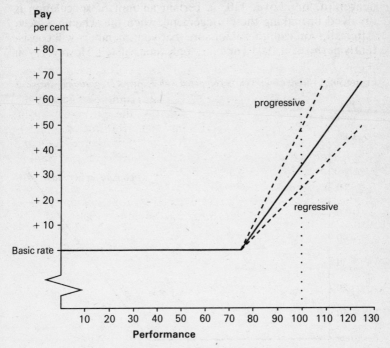

Consultants and employers have produced a number of complex schemes with which to baffle members, stewards and full-time officers. Some, when drawn on a graph, reveal amazing bends, curves and dog-legs and it is difficult to believe that their purpose is other than to deceive. If you are offered a bonus scheme where performance and earnings are shown in table form, the essential first step is to **compare** it with straight-proportional by drawing both on a piece of graph paper. The graph should be drawn up as shown in Figure 27: the vertical scale shows earnings either as percentages of the basic rate or in real money terms (whichever is convenient); the bottom line shows the performance index (PI).

The key area to examine is the range between 90 PI and 110 PI, as the average worker's performance, once acclimatised to incentive working, is likely to be between those two figures. In fact, the average performance after a year or two may well be nearer to, or above, 110. A certain amount of speculation is involved in making these judgements when the scheme is new. After all, you cannot say for sure that your members will consistently perform at 100 PI or over – only time will tell. However, you

Figure 30: *A variable bonus curve compared with a straight proportional scheme*

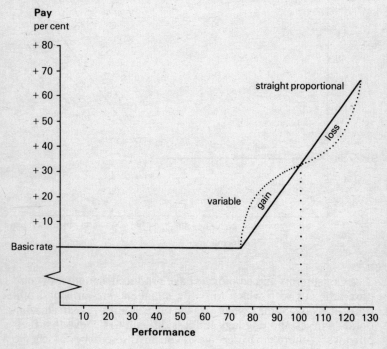

The variable scheme is consistently more rewarding financially up to a 99 performance. Beyond 100 it becomes an absurd confidence trick.

can spot the traps in advance and explain them to the membership, who may feel that a trial period is in order.

Many schemes offered by consultants incorporate a 'sprat to catch a mackerel', in that the scheme looks better than straight-proportional for peformances between 75 PI and 100 PI, but not so good above 100 PI. In these circumstances it is probably a reasonably safe bet to assume that the consultant expects to see the average worker performing above 100 PI before too long; Figure 30 illustrates one example involving a bonus curve instead of a straight line.

10.
Stability of earnings

Bonus percentages / overtime and shift premiums / work booking / 'faulty' work / holidays and sick pay / summary of chapters 7–10 / checklist on chapters 7–10

No incentive bonus scheme can really provide consistent earnings without consistent output, and that depends much more on employers and governments than it does on the attitudes and application of the workers concerned. Workers do not control the employer's sales policy, market strategy, production scheduling or long-term planning, all of which affect the work available. In reality, incentive schemes offer workers as much discretion in their working lives as is offered to a rat sniffing out a morsel of food in a laboratory maze.

In addition to the broad factors mentioned above, there are others of a more local nature which have similar effects upon the work available, such as material shortages, customer demand and management inefficiency. Moreover, long-term movements in basic rates, and the negotiating policies of unions and employers, often have a direct bearing on bonus earnings and gross pay.

Chapter 2 dealt with one immediate source of income fluctuation – the payments made for waiting time and unmeasured work. This chapter examines some of the **longer-term** pay issues which will also need to be covered in an incentive scheme agreement.

Bonus percentages

A simple rule to follow when drawing up bonus tables is *never* to allow the bonus for each level of performance to be stated in pounds and pence. Bonus levels should always be stated as percentages of the basic rate so that bonus earnings retain their true value when basic rates are increased. There are exceptions to this rule where the membership has developed a positive strategy to gradually eliminate the incentive scheme; this exception will be covered later. Figure 31 shows what happens to gross earnings after a basic rate increase, when bonus earnings are expressed in cash terms and not as percentages of the basic rate.

Figure 31: *The declining value of a cash bonus*

Year	Negotiated basic rate increase %	Basic rate	Cash bonus at standard performance	Bonus %	Actual increase in gross pay %
1978	—	£60.00	£20.00	33.3	—
1979	15	£69.00	£20.00	29	11.3
1980	20	£82.80	£20.00	24.2	15.5
1981	10	£91.08	£20.00	22	8.1
1982	6	£96.54	£20.00	20.7	4.9

Clearly, schemes which state bonus payments in cash terms quickly become regressive, unless additional negotiations maintain standard bonus at one-third of the basic rate. The table also shows that the actual increase in gross pay is *lower* than the percentage increase negotiated.

This problem has been faced by workers in many industries, notably engineering and printing, where employers have insisted on paying bonus earnings as a percentage of the nationally-agreed minimum basic rate despite the fact that locally-agreed basic rates are much higher. In other cases, increases have been negotiated as 'supplements' so that they do not affect the basic rates used to calculate bonus earnings or overtime premiums. This led to the growth of what became known as the '*bonus calculator rate*', a rate which lost all connection with the basic rate.

Similar conditions were imposed by governments between 1969 and 1979, when, having encouraged the growth of productivity and incentive schemes throughout the sixties and seventies, they became aware of the bonus 'roll-up' effect which meant that a pound on the basic rate put £1.30 to £1.60 on the gross pay. Pay policies were then designed to allow employers to renege on earlier agreements covering incentive schemes.

Overtime and shift premiums

Premium payments for unsocial hours, either through shift-working or overtime, are such a common feature of collective agreements that they hardly seem worth commenting upon. The pattern of payments varies from industry to industry, but it is rare to find anyone prepared to work overtime for less than time plus a quarter, or for less than double-time on Sundays. Similarly, shift premiums vary from cash supplements to strict formulae, such as time plus a third or time plus a half, depending upon the industry and the strength of local bargaining.

In most cases, trade unionists have insisted upon these payments being set not in cash terms but as fractions or percentages of the basic rate, thus ensuring that the premiums retain their real value when the basic rate is increased. This lesson has often been learned the hard way, yet, when incentive bonus schemes are negotiated, the lesson seems to be forgotten. Employers are allowed, by default, to cut the shift rate, cut the overtime rate and, in some cases, pay overtime premiums which are barely above the day rate. This bizarre state of affairs is made possible through the inherent deception in the psychology of bonus schemes – the presentation of bonus earnings as 'something extra', a handout for hard work.

For years, this little trick enabled employers to avoid paying bonus earnings to pieceworkers during holiday periods. Although few organised workers would allow that to happen today, they still permit employers to use the 'something extra' fraud as a means of cutting traditional premium payments. In practice, what employers do is to avoid paying overtime and shift premiums on that part of **normal** pay which is made up by bonus earnings. The effect is to reduce those premiums below the level negotiated, as shown by the example in Figure 32.

Figure 32: *The premium fraud*

	Hourly basic rate	Standard bonus at 33.3%	Gross hourly pay	Shift premium at time + ½ of basic pay	Shift premium as a % of gross pay
No bonus scheme	£1.50	nil	£1.50	£0.75	50
Scheme working	£1.50	£0.50	£2.00	£0.75	37.5

To further illustrate this fraud, we can look at what happens to unit labour costs. Take the example of a worker producing, say, 15 units per hour for a basic hourly rate of £1.50 – labour costs are 10p per unit. When that same worker moves onto overtime at time plus a half, 15 units per hour are still produced but this time for £2.25 (£1.50 plus £0.75) – labour costs have now risen to 15p per unit. The employer is usually quite happy to pay this extra sum as the overhead costs on overtime are significantly reduced.

When that same worker moves onto a straight-proportional bonus scheme paying a bonus of one-third of the basic rate at standard performance, there is very little apparent change at first. Output will rise by at least one-third to 20 units per hour and the hourly rate to £2.00 (£1.50 basic plus £0.50 bonus) – labour costs are still 10p per unit. However, when the incentive worker moves onto overtime at time plus a half, the employer gains further savings. Output will still be constant at 20 units per hour, but hourly earnings will rise to £2.75 (£1.50 basic, plus £0.50 bonus, plus £0.75 premium) – labour costs are now 13.75p per unit; less than was being paid before the scheme was introduced.

This is by no means the worst situation that can occur. Some schemes, notably in the National Health Service, do not allow bonus earnings to be paid on overtime at all. Workers covered by some NHS agreements move from basic rate plus one-third during normal hours to basic rate plus one-half during overtime – an overtime premium of 12.5%!

Whether there will be any overtime left to do, once the incentive scheme is introduced and operating, is another matter. One of the employer's main aims in proposing work study and incentives will be to **eliminate overtime** as far as possible. It could be said that this is not necessarily a bad thing but, if the elimination of overtime does not lead to more jobs and if it is carried out in a way which sells the workers short, it becomes difficult to see much 'good' in the exercise. Bearing in mind that the employer will be expecting an increase in output of, at the very least, one-third where standard time-based incentives are introduced for the first time, it is immediately obvious that the increased pace of work produces an extra 13 hours' capacity per worker (one-third of a normal 40-hour week). This is enough to effectively wipe out Saturday working plus an evening or two where this has been the employer's only way of increasing output.

How does the average worker fare in this deal? To find out,

we can take a hypothetical but not unusual example. One of the most common agreements covering Saturday overtime working where the normal week is Monday to Friday, is for the time to be paid at time plus a half for the first 4 hours and double time thereafter. This means than an 8-hour Saturday is worth 14 hours pay at basic rate; 14 extra hours' pay as a percentage of the normal 40 hours pay is 35%. By working on Saturday, the employer's capacity is increased by 8 hours to 48 hours; an increase of 20%. So, to increase capacity by 20% through offering Saturday overtime the employer increases labour costs by 35%. The introduction of work study and associated incentive schemes will increase output by 33% to 70%, whilst increasing labour costs by only 33.3% at standard performance! In effect, the employer shifts the extra earnings paid on overtime to form part of the normal week's pay and swaps a 20% increase in capacity for something far higher.

If the employer can also contrive to deny indirect service workers a similar increase in pay (as many do), there is an added bonus for the employer as the former overtime earnings of the service workers go straight into the employer's pocket, along with any other savings made through not opening the plant on Saturdays.

This criticism is not in defence of overtime working nor is it an attack upon the strategy of reducing working hours to create jobs. It is, however, critical of the muddled thinking which allows the expression of pious sentiments about the evil of overtime while having no similar reservations about the consequences of incentive working.

Work Booking

Procedures for booking work and allocating time will also change as a result of work study. In some cases, the system will be **computerised**. In order to calculate bonus earnings for an individual or a group of workers, the work study office or works cashier will need information on output, SMVs for each type of output, productive time, waiting time, unmeasured work and actual attendance hours. Normally this information will be booked and entered by the workers concerned and, perhaps, checked or countersigned by a supervisor. It is customary for bonus earnings to be paid one week in arrears, which means that there can be quite a memory-erasing delay between completing a work sheet and receiving the bonus.

It is essential to have procedures for checking that the bonus has been properly calculated and that work bookings have not been tampered with by management. Many workplaces appoint a 'bonus steward' who has sufficient time away from normal work to deal with queries and to check calculations. By itself this is not enough; the bonus steward can hardly be expected to know what every member has booked every day of the week. The system also has the weakness of throwing the responsibility onto one person's shoulders instead of where it belongs – with each individual member. An effective checking system must start from the principle that no member of management is permitted to alter any individual's work recording without that individual's consent, given in the presence of a union representative. If management wish to challenge any work recordings or if they believe that any are incorrect, this procedure must be followed. Substantial bonus earnings can be lost when members of line management decide that four hours booked to 'waiting' should be amended to two hours, or when unmeasured work is claimed which mysteriously becomes waiting time.

The second requirement is for the work study office to publish all calculations for the previous day's work within 24 hours; that is before memories have grown dim. These figures should be given to each individual or group, or posted on the workplace notice board. In this sense it is not authoritarian for the union representatives to cast their eye over work recordings, as some members may be having considerable trouble in getting to grips with the scheme. It may also be a good idea for union representatives to keep an eye on the general levels of waiting time and unmeasured work, particularly where these activities are not paid at average performance.

The simplification of workers' jobs and the development of cheap technology has enabled management to effectively tie many workers to their work station, with their movements and output booked by computer. The 'black box' or 'spy in the cab', which may be introduced into the road haulage industry, can just as easily be attached to factory machinery. The recordings over a day would show when the machinery was running, for how long and at what speed. Work can also be issued to operatives by computer. An order received by the factory can be converted by the production control department into a standard time, using the data collected through work study, and placed in a queue on the central computer along with all the other information about the job which the operative will require. For example, a turner or miller in the engineering industry would need to know the precise specifications of the piece to be produced, details on metal quality and tolerances as well as information on parts and tools to be drawn from the stores. If the job in question is done often enough, all this information can be stored on the computer and reissued with each future order. The operative, on completing a job, simply receives the next job from a computer terminal in the engineering shop. As the next job is taken, the computer will record who took the job, when it was taken and the expected time of completion, which can be calculated through the use of standard times.

Of course, these systems can be introduced with or without work study but they are of little use to management unless there is some method of assessing job times and of ensuring that workers keep to the times set. Work study and incentive schemes provide this vital ingredient.

'Faulty' work

Many incentive scheme agreements contain a clause which enables the employer to penalise workers who produce faulty or unsatisfactory work. This normally takes the form of withholding or deducting all performance credits for work which is deemed to be faulty, as in this typical clause from an agreement in the construction industry:

> No performance will be credited for work which is faulty or sub-standard. Faulty work will be made good by those responsible with no allowance for the time involved. Where faulty work has to be rectified by others, the bonus earned on rectification will be deducted from those originally responsible.

As you can imagine, this type of clause is a recipe for all kinds of dispute – including disputes between workers. The clause does not say *who* is to decide whether work is sub-standard, nor does it contain any procedure for deciding *why* work is sub-standard; it also omits any kind of **appeals procedure**. The cause of the faulty work may lie in poor quality materials, bad working conditions, lack of correct tools and equipment, insufficient or incorrect information about the job – the list is virtually endless. Yet, whatever the cause, the agreement quoted above would ensure that the worker or workers concerned are financially penalised.

At least the code or requirements for National Health Service incentive schemes does state that the deduction of performance credits will only apply 'if the faulty work is definitely attributable to the member of staff or group concerned and in no way results from factors outside their control'. This clause ensures that the employer has to **prove** the case before imposing a deduction in pay.

Financial penalties for 'faulty' work are a further example of the curious lapses in consciousness to which even militant trade unionists are prone when involved in incentive schemes.

If bonus earnings are regarded as 'pay' and not as 'something extra', it makes no sense to extort pay penalties for sub-standard or faulty work. Would we expect a typist who makes a mess of a letter to pay for the paper used? Should a bus driver pay for damage to a bus where he or she is at fault? Do managers cough up the cost of their own bad decisions? Faulty work will occur and sometimes it will be caused by the actions of a particular worker or group of workers. We all make mistakes from time to time and we all experience the occasional off-days. Sufficient research has been carried out to argue that work organisation itself (including the effects of incentive working) produces intolerable stress, tension and frustration which, obviously, affect workers' attitudes to work and manner of working – you will find a greater risk of ulcers on the shopfloor and in the office than you will in the boardroom.

Holidays and sick pay

The practice of excluding bonus payments from the calculation of holiday pay and sick pay is much less common than it was in the sixties. It should not be necessary to make out a case for including average bonus earnings in all pay-related benefits, including pension entitlement, but these issues can be overlooked. The most common procedure, where bonus earnings are allowed to fluctuate week by week in relation to performance, is to calculate an **average bonus level** over a period, usually 13 weeks.

The length of the calculation period is a matter for negotiation in each circumstance but it should not be too short, and, thereby, run the risk of holiday pay for the next 12 months being based upon a 'bad' month. It is probably most sensible to agree a reference period for the calculation of average bonus which will apply to every worker equally, and to maintain the agreed average for a year. Of course, averages can rise and fall over 12 months, so there will still be an element of 'swings and roundabouts'. If an average bonus is calculated for the purpose of determining sick pay and holiday pay, it will need to be updated from time to time to reflect any movements in basic pay.

For example, take the worker whose basic pay is £2.00 per hour in July and whose average bonus (based upon the reference period of April, May and June) is £0.80. Assuming there are no other payments to be included, this worker would receive £2.80 per hour for all holidays taken between July this year and July next year. This is quite workable until there is a change in basic rates negotiated at national level or local level. If bonus payments are based upon a percentage of the basic rate, it will not be enough to simply include the new increase in the holiday rate. In this ex-ample, the worker's bonus at 80 pence per hour, represents 40% of the basic hourly rate. If, during the course of the next 12 months, the basic rate is increased, then the agreement must allow for the average bonus to maintain its value at 40% of the *new* basic rate. If this is not done then taking holidays will incur a wage cut.

The simplest method of overcoming this problem is to state the average bonus over the reference period as a percentage of the basic rate, leaving the actual cash sum to be calculated when each holiday is taken. The same arguments apply to sick pay, bank holidays and paid time off for union duties.

An alternative is to pay each worker as though he or she was actually at work that week; that is, at the same rates as their colleagues. However, this involves some element of retrospective pay, as holiday pay is always paid in advance and it is not possible to predict accurately, in every case, what the bonus of each work group will be.

Summary of Chapters 7-10

■ The general terms of the incentive scheme will be covered in a main agreement, sometimes called a **'work specification part one'**.

■ In large plants, a supplementary agreement called a **'work specification part two'** may be drawn up for each department.

■ The part two will usually detail a list of **duties** and job descriptions of the workers in the department and a table of **standard minute values** (SMVs).

■ Some activities will *not* be given an SMV; these include **waiting time** and **unmeasured work** and, possibly one or two additional categories.

■ A **performance index** (PI) will be agreed for all activities other than measured work (work for which an SMV has been agreed).

■ Performance will usually be calculated **weekly** for each worker or group of workers, based upon the following factors:

    a) attendance time;

    b) time spent on measured work;

    c) sms earned on measured work;

    d) time spent on waiting; and

    e) time spent on unmeasured activities.

■ The performance credits for all measured and unmeasured activities are usually **averaged** over the attendance time in each week, to arrive at a performance index for the whole week.

■ The weekly performance index is read off against a chart to find the **bonus payment** for that week for all attendance hours.

    Example: 99 PI = 31.1% of basic rate

               100 PI = 33.3% of basic rate

               101 PI = 35.5% of basic rate

■ The **amount** of bonus paid for each level of performance is entirely a matter for negotiation.

■ Most trade unionists insist that bonus schemes should be **straight-proportional** or better, with a mutually agreed bonus ceiling.

Checklist on Chapters 7-10

■ Working at incentive pace yields productivity improvements on top of those already made through new work methods, new equipment and elimination of old customs and practices – do you know what **productivity increases** have been achieved by these changes?

■ Have you sufficient information and statistics on output and working hours *before* work study was introduced to enable **comparisons** to be made?

■ Do your members **understand** the scheme and the method of calculating performance and pay? Will each member receive a **copy** of the agreement? Have management agreed to allow full department meetings in works time so that members can **discuss** the issues with their representatives?

■ Is it a condition of the scheme that **daily** and **weekly statistics** on output, working hours, sms earned, waiting time, unmeasured work and bonus calculations will be provided?

■ Have you sufficient facilities to **file** this information? (They may become very useful in the future.)

■ Your members' earnings wil be calculated according to the time and work which they book; can management **alter work bookings** without the member's or steward's approval?

■ Is the scheme **straight-proportional** or better? Have you made comparisons?

■ Is the bonus for each level of performance stated as a **percentage** of the basic rate and not in cash?

■ Will **overtime** and **shift premiums** be applied to bonus earnings as well as to the basic rate?

■ Will waiting time and unmeasured activities be credited at **average** performance?

■ Will **average** bonus be paid in holiday and sick pay?

■ Will bonus earnings be based upon **group** or **individual** performances? (See Chapter 12.)

11.
Measured day work (MDW)

'Stepped' or 'banded' MDW / MDW and job
evaluation / job evaluation and collective
bargaining / why job evaluation?

As a straight system of payment there is not a great deal to be
explained about measured day work. The arguments which raged
around its introduction, particularly in the engineering industry,
have had more to do with the issue of day-to-day control than with
cash. At its simplest, MDW can be introduced following work
measurement as an alternative to the type of scheme discussed in
the previous chapters, where bonus earnings fluctuate week by
week according to the performance achieved.

In its simple form, MDW involves setting a target performance and agreeing a consolidated 'day rate' for the target
performance. Workers are not required or expected to exceed the
target performance, nor are they expected to be consistently
below the target. The question of rewards for above-target performance and penalties for under-achievement is entirely a matter
for negotiation. Some schemes allow for four or five levels of
performance, each with its own day rate and, usually, workers
who fail to achieve their target over a period are warned before
their earnings are affected.

One of the main attractions of most MDW schemes to trade
unionists is the removal of all unmeasured activities from performance calculations, so that the assessment of a worker's
performance is based solely upon the measured work which he or
she is given to do. This is not necessarily the case with all MDW
schemes; for example, those used in local authorities and the
health service still incorporate waiting time and unmeasured work
in performance calculations. These schemes are not really MDW
in its widely-accepted form but represent a standard time-based
incentive scheme modified to produce consistent performances
each week instead of fluctuating performances. There were two
reasons for their introduction into the health service. Firstly,

management were not at all interested in workers having the incentive to increase their output as and when they felt fit; hospitals have a finite amount of work to be done and any increase in output by one worker simply means that there is less to be done by the other members of the group. Secondly, by agreeing a fixed level of performance, the NHS management were retaining control over the scheme.

With a few exceptions, MDW is basically an **agreed level of pay** for an **agreed level of performance** on measured work, even if the time spent on measured work is reduced by waiting time or other interruptions. It would seem that MDW can overcome the problems of fluctuating income levels through factors beyond the workers' control. It can also be an effective check upon virtuoso speed merchants who care more for their own wage packet than they do for group solidarity.

The fundamental problem with MDW is usually the complete assumption of control by management over output levels and methods of work. The key to understanding this issue is the fact that **output** is not the same as **performance** in work study terms. To re-cap on what performance actually means it is necessary to recall how standard times are set. The standard time for a task is based upon three things:

a) the observed time;
b) the rating; and
c) the relaxation allowances.

The result is the time for a task based upon standard **effort** being applied by the worker. Standard performance, therefore, means standard effort and *not* standard output; MDW offers consistent earnings for consistent **effort**. What this means in practice is that any MDW scheme still requires standard times to be set and still involves the same wrangles over rating and allowances.

However, now that both sides are committed to fairly consistent earnings, the twist comes when new work methods are introduced. For example, a car worker's job consists of fitting the front seat to a particular model of car for which the standard time is 5 sms. Assuming that the agreed level of performance under the MDW scheme is 100 (standard), then 12 seats will have to be fitted in each hour of measured work. Suppose that management subsequently modifies that particular car model, which affects the seat design and the method of fitting. After re-study and measurement of the altered method, the standard time is re-issued at 4 sms – 15 seats per hour instead of 12. The basis of the revised standard time will again be the observed time, the rating and the relaxation allowances. Management will point out that the reduced time and resulting increase in the worker's productivity have been made possible by simplifying and improving the component and the work method – the worker's **effort** remains the same although output has been increased by 25%.

The principle of MDW (and, for that matter, of work study) has not been violated; the same effort gets the same reward, despite the fact that the average car worker smells a rat. The issue at stake is precisely the same as in any system based upon work measurement; that is, whether trade unionists will allow management to increase output and productivity, by changing work methods or the product, without having to meet some claim for an improvement in terms and conditions.

The reason MDW caused immense problems in the engineering industry, and the car industry in particular, was that it replaced the old **piecework system**, usually in the face of strong protests by the unions. One of the conditions of the old system was that all piece rates had to be mutually agreed. This provision enabled the stewards to bargain over every change which occurred, and ensured that management could not push through changes in design and methods to the workers' detriment. This was one of the main sources of trade-union control at the workplace; when the piecework system was smashed and replaced by MDW, local control enforced by the steward was bypassed.

The crux of the problem was that although the old system obliged management to negotiate over piece rates, which could effectively delay any new models, or alterations to existing models, until agreement was reached, the actual work methods were not a major issue. Once management had, apparently, removed the threat of loss of earnings by offering a consistent level of pay through MDW, they had not only eliminated an important source of worker controls but had also seized total control of work **methods**. In many areas of the engineering industry, there are no effective status quo agreements through which workers can demand the right to reject any changes which are not mutually agreed. The result is that, although stewards may object to a new standard time which is issued following a method or model change, the process of negotiation ends right there. The only way in which the validity of a particular standard time can be checked is, not surprisingly, through further studies taken by a work study engineer using the rules of work study. Of course, this is the reason why MDW was introduced by management in the first place.

In the late sixties, British Leyland succeeded in imposing MDW on sections of their workforce with the implied threat of a lock-out, after the engineering unions had struggled to retain the piecework system. The then president of the AEU, Hugh Scanlon, claimed that piecework gave workers a measure of control over their own efforts and earnings which should be defended. While this is true, the control which management most objected to was the right to say 'no' to arbitrary change which the mutuality clause gave to the stewards. So, the major issue with MDW was not the change from one **payment system** to another but the surrender of **control** to management.

It is important to make this distinction, as a move to MDW does not *necessarily* entail the elimination of status quo agreements, whether written or maintained by custom and practice. This failure to distinguish the important aspects of piecework from the unimportant, has led to a number of trade unionists and sympathetic academics to support piecework as a means of maintaining or extending workers' controls. Some pro-worker commentators have claimed that it was the existence of the piecework system, and the importance of the role of the steward under that system, which fostered the tremendous struggle by the workers at Gardner's Diesels in opposing mass redundancies in 1980. This is hardly a careful analysis of the situation; it is perfectly possible to have piecework *without* status quo and it is also perfectly possible to have MDW *with* status quo. The issue is one of control and not one of the method of calculating pay.

This problem is present wherever employers are free to introduce change aimed at increasing productivity without having to reach agreement with the employees first; work study is a sophisticated and complex procedure, with all the appearances of fairness, offering the principle of reward based solely upon effort. Its application in MDW is no worse than that in more conventional standard time-based incentive schemes – in both cases, management are presented with an opportunity to suppress or eliminate collective bargaining over change and productivity.

Yet this does not have to be the case. Some of the positive aspects of MDW can be utilised to provide a degree of income security, such as a guaranteed level of pay, the abolition of competition between workers over output targets and pay packets, and the elimination of waiting time as a factor affecting pay. To those who argue that any link between output and pay is unacceptable, it should be pointed out that in almost all workplaces, even in the absence of incentive schemes, there is some notional level of a day's work. It may not exist officially or be written into an agreement, but it can be enforced by management through the dismissal or harassment of 'unsatisfactory' workers. Similarly, it may be enforced by workers through self-imposed limits on output – most workers and work groups know what constitutes 'enough'. Provided that a strong trade-union organisation has been developed, with the membership fully aware of the importance of the principle of status quo, and prepared to defend it, the move from more traditional incentive schemes to MDW need not be as traumatic as that experienced by the automobile workers.

Perhaps the major problem for local union representatives is the size and scope of the actual MDW agreement itself, and the way it can affect traditional negotiating arrangements. Most MDW schemes are **plant-wide** in their application and structure. This means that, while standard times and methods may be negotiated department-by-department with the particular representatives and members directly involved, the rules for calculating those standards will be stated in a plant agreement. This shifts the emphasis away from local group bargaining to plant or even national level negotiations. The membership loses much of the control it may have had over day-to-day issues, such as rest allowances and production targets, because individual stewards are not allowed to negotiate changes in the plant agreement. Management will have ensured that the plant agreement contains procedures which permit method changes, new studies and amendments to existing standard times. The corresponding procedures for members and their representatives are usually confined to challenging the accuracy of any new studies. The overall effect is to make it much more difficult to raise new bargaining issues when management propose change at work.

'Stepped' or 'banded' MDW

These schemes, which are a variation on the simplest form of MDW, set a **number** of performance and pay 'bands' as a substitute for one simple, overall performance target. If a group of workers accepts a simple MDW scheme with a standard (100 on the BSI 0–100 scale) target performance, their basic rate will be combined with an element of bonus which is fixed, to produce a new 'day rate'. The day rate does not fluctuate so there is no incentive to perform above standard and management has disciplinary problems with those workers who consistently perform below standard.

For these reasons, 'stepped' or 'banded' schemes have been developed. **Stepped MDW** can provide as many as seven or eight pay and performance levels. For example, if the day rate for standard performance is £112 per week, made up of £84 basic plus one-third (£28) as the bonus element, employers might like to add a pay level either side of standard. This would provide an incentive to fast workers and a penalty to those unable to regularly achieve standard.

This is most commonly done by establishing a performance 'band' of, say, 98 to 102 inclusive. All performances within this band would be paid at the £112 per week rate so that workers who perform at 98 and 99 are receiving the full pay benefits of a standard performance; those working at 101 and 102 are being underpaid.

A performance band covering the range 93 to 97 and another covering the range from 103 to 107 can be added either side of the standard band. The day rate for the higher band would probably be based upon a 105 performance – the middle of the band (£84 × 105 ÷ 75 = £117.60); and the rate for the lower band based upon a performance of 95 (£84 × 95 ÷ 75 = £106.40).

Once this particular ball has started rolling, performance bands can grow either side of standard, like this:

band A	83 – 87 =	£95.20 (85)
band B	88 – 92 =	£100.80 (90)
band C	93 – 98 =	£106.40 (95)
band D	99 – 102 =	£112.00 (100)
band E	103 – 107 =	£117.60 (105)
band F	108 – 112 =	£123.20 (110)

The actual number of performance and pay bands, their ranges and payment levels, are a matter for negotiation. Each band could have a range of ten performance points with the payment level set at the top, or towards the top, of each band instead of the centre.

The rules governing the way people move up and down the

performance and pay bands are also negotiable. Most commonly, workers who *raise* their performance to a level above the one they normally occupy are immediately paid at the higher of the two bands. Rewards are immediate while penalties are slower to have effect. Workers who drop a band are not immediately penalised financially but warned instead. A failure to put their performance 'right' over the next week or two brings about the inevitable wage cut – usually after two consecutive warnings. The fact that employers are quick to reward 'improvements' in performance says a lot about the benefits they derive from high bonus earners, as well as the psychology they employ.

In the National Health Service, which favours banded MDW schemes, the problems of raising performances are much more aggressively stated. In the NHS, each work group has to agree to move from the contracted pay band for the whole group, should such a change be desired. The consequences for each work group are usually baldly stated; as there is a finite amount of work available for the group, an increase in pay and performance must be met by a reduction in the number of jobs in that group. The jobs lost then pay for the increased earnings of those remaining – this is management control through incentive schemes at its purest.

Many employers have already made the shift from fluctuating incentive schemes based upon standard times, to some system of MDW; many more will attempt to do so in the future. Local authority direct works departments are already under close scrutiny. The employers' reasons for the change, apart from those already mentioned, include the fact that almost any incentive scheme eventually outlives its usefulness to the employer, often because the workers involved gradually gain a degree of control over the scheme's workings. MDW not only presents the employer with an opportunity to regain control but it also provides an ingredient essential to forward planning – **consistency**.

For trade unionists, one of the side benefits of work measurement schemes is the amount of information generated on output, working hours and labour costs. Provided that this information is available to union representatives, it may provide a useful back-up in future negotiations on changes proposed by management, including new technology. When employers start to make noises about 'new' schemes or 'time for a change', don't throw out the baby with the bathwater – hang on to those old weekly performance sheets and output analyses, they may be useful.

MDW and job evaluation

Where measured day work is introduced to replace existing incentive schemes, **job evaluation** often comes with it, hand-in-hand. Employers may present the combination of the two techniques as a 'fresh start' and as a way of sorting out old problems. The apparent attractions of job evaluation for trade unionists are various. Some groups of workers may feel that their skills have been consistently under-valued compared to other groups; some may believe that they have suffered because of a lack of bargaining power; others could be convinced that their case has been ignored by both management and union representatives. Add to this a wide range of possible pay levels covering overtime, bonus schemes, and odd agreements here and there, and you have a nightmare of wage anomalies to which job evaluation appears to offer a solution.

Unless ironed out, these anomalies may destroy any 'fresh start' which management tries to introduce. Management must be seen to be fair to everybody, so job evaluation is dressed up as a neutral method of achieving fairness in the shape of a new wage structure. Job evaluation is as manipulative and biased as work study and, in many cases, drives another nail into the coffin of collective bargaining. It is not necessary to go into job evaluation in *detail* here, but, because of its assocation with MDW, it requires a brief description.

Methods of job evaluation

Firstly, job evaluation is used to evaluate the **job** not the **job holder**. The methods used can be simple and straightforward, like organising all jobs into an agreed number of grades on a 'felt fair' basis, or they can be slightly more complex, involving job factors and points scoring. (I say '*slightly* more complex', because no job evaluation system is really difficult to understand – they are made to look difficult by consultants who rely on this *apparent* complexity to make a living.)

Job evaluation can involve a few union representatives, a pencil and a piece of paper or it can take a consultant, reams of paper and a computer. The objective is just the same – to come up with a workable wage structure. There are only three management tests for a 'workable' wage structure:

a) How much will it cost to introduce?
b) Will the workforce accept it? and
c) How long will it last?

Anything outside these issues is pure window dressing.

The more complex and so-called 'analytical' methods of job evaluation usually involve the following:

a) detailed job **descriptions** of each job;
b) an examination of each job against a set of job characteristics, usually called **job factors**;
c) a system of scoring **points** for each job factor; and
d) arranging all jobs into an **order** based upon the points **total** each job has scored.

Job descriptions

Job descriptions usually list the **actual work** involved in the job, any particular **knowledge** or **skill** required and the degree of **responsibility** undertaken. They can be as detailed or as simple as you want them to be, but compiling them provides management with some useful information and the opportunity to add a few extra responsibilities to some jobs, or to take a few away. They also create a pool of information which management could find useful in any future job disputes.

Job factors

These may vary from employer to employer and from one firm of consultants to another. The most common job factors are:

a) education/training;
b) responsibility;
c) skill; and
d) working environment.

Some consultants may split the factor 'skill' into 'mental skills' (planning, calculating, etc.), 'physical skills' (dexterity etc.) and 'social skills' (working with others, communicating, etc.). All sorts of sub-factors are possible and the list is endless, however, the four factors quoted above are in general use and are sufficient to enable any job to be evaluated by scoring points against each factor.

Points rating (scoring)

There is no fixed system of points rating but the objective is the same in all cases. The procedure involves allocating a score against each job factor for each and every job, so that each job eventually acquires a points total which will determine its position in the organisation's 'pay league' or wage structure. One simple method is to grade each job factor against five degrees of difficulty;

high	5 points
above average	4 points
average	3 points
below average	2 points
low	1 point

With the above system, a job which scored 'high' on the **skill** factor, 'above average' on the **education** and **responsibility** factors, and 'low' on **working environment**, would amass a total of 14 points. If the procedure was that simple and innocent, little more would remain to be said. Unfortunately, job evaluation systems involve some substantial 'doctoring' along the way.

Weighting

Weighting is the first and most obvious 'doctoring' which occurs. To illustrate, we can take just two job factors – **skill** and **working environment**, and assume that points are scored against each factor using the points system described above. A mucky job, requiring considerable physical effort, scores five on **working environment** but only one point for **skill**; a total of six points. A different job, requiring technical qualifications but carried out in the comfort of an air-conditioned office, also scores six points but in the opposite fashion. We can only conclude from this that both jobs are 'equal' and should be paid at the same rate. In practice, most employers would keep clerical and manual jobs apart under separate schemes, but the question still arises when grading or evaluating a wide range of manual work – do we treat work carried out in unpleasant conditions equally with skilled work undertaken in a more comfortable environment?

Because most people would suggest skill is more valuable than physical effort or working in dirt, the points awarded under the job factor **skill** are 'weighted', that is, given extra value. This is achieved by multiplying the scores under certain job factors.

Typically, points awarded under **education** and **responsibility** might be increased by a multiplier of two (doubled), and **skill** by one and a half. **Working environment** might be left unweighted, or even halved.

The effect of weighting, in most job evaluation schemes, is to inflate the points scored for mental and managerial type jobs, while playing down the scores for those jobs of an unskilled or more physical nature. Consultants would argue that weighting helps to produce job scores in line with most people's expectations and that, unless the final wage structure satisfies people's expectations, it will not be acceptable or even workable. Given the way society is currently ordered, this is true, but it hardly allows the term 'neutral' to be applied to job evaluation.

Weighting reveals bias and manipulation at its most obvious. There are less obvious methods of inflating the scores of certain types of jobs, such as:

■ scoring **responsibility** from 0–20 while scoring **skill** from 0–10; or

■ including several sub-factors under **responsibility**, such as: responsibility for the work of others; responsibility for implementing management policy; and responsibility for machinery, while providing no sub-factors under **working environment**. If the maximum score for a sub-factor is five points, **responsibility** has a maximum of 15, while **working environment** remains at five – before weighting is even applied.

Even the four basic job factors we have been looking at include a subtle piece of manipulation. It seems that jobs which require some formal educational achievement, whether a degree or an apprenticeship, can score points against that factor. Additional points are then awarded for actually *using* the skills which that education provided. This is like giving a bus driver five points for holding a driving licence and a further five for being able to drive.

Job evaluation and collective bargaining

Whatever ranking system is used, jobs are usually sorted into grades or bands of jobs with similar scores. The wage for each grade is entirely a matter for negotiation. This involves setting a differential between each grade. The more grades you have, the more difficult the negotiations will be – especially where several unions are involved. Stewards who launch into this exercise without a clear strategy agreed between all groups of workers could damage trade-union solidarity for years to come.

Job evaluation often involves trade-union participation in compiling job descriptions and job scores and in some kind of appeals panel. This, it is argued, makes the system democratic – so long as the rules of the system are unchallenged. Once job evaluation has been carried out and the results implemented, those same rules continue to operate and to restrict collective bargaining. Management will strongly resist any claim which they see as disrupting the wage structure.

The twin pincers of measured day work and job evaluation cut out almost all the issues which are not covered by the rules of either scheme. If new machinery or equipment is introduced, MDW takes care of overall pay issues so that productivity and output take a back seat to effort. If stewards argue that the new machinery requires greater skill or responsibility on the part of their members, then the job evaluation scheme will reduce that argument to a question of assessing how many points are involved, and whether any increased score is sufficient to move that job into the next grade.

Most new technology has the effect of reducing skill and responsibility while output is raised without increased effort. If stewards cannot mount an effective argument over **productivity** (which is ignored by both MDW and job evaluation), any claims they wish to make on behalf of the membership will be difficult to substantiate.

Why job evaluation?

Job evaluation seldom brings any important alterations to existing wage relativities. Management emerge at the top and women usually remain at the bottom. The system is based entirely on the reinforcement of existing prejudices ('people's expectations'). How can it be otherwise? To be workable, any new wage structure must reflect the dominant values in this society. These demand that education and skill should attract financial reward; that responsibility should be taken away from the many and given to the few, who are then rewarded for accepting it.

Against this it can be argued that jobs which offer satisfaction or freedom to exercise one's creativity and initiative, ought to be scored down, while jobs which are de-skilled and monotonous should be uprated. The idea that boring jobs should attract rewards similar to those of more satisfying work appear to stand the world on its head. However, if assembly line workers were paid the same as doctors, you would not find many members of the medical profession queueing at Ford's.

It is perfectly understandable that workers and their representatives desire a sense of fairness in pay relationships. Pursuing leap-frog claims, fighting for some kind of justice for the low paid, consistently seeing work underrated if it is done by women, watching small groups with strong bargaining power move ahead of the 'pack', posing worker against worker, makes for a fairly tiresome way of life. Job evaluation has nothing to do with justice and cannot put these wrongs to right.

As trade unionists we need to ask ourselves what *we* want from a wage structure and what kind of payment system suits *our* needs. If solidarity is important in workplace struggles, why not have just three rates of pay – or even two? Does it really suit our needs to allow workers to be carved up into sectional interest groups? Pay relativities and differentials would become far less important as bargaining issues, if trade unions directed greater attention to the jobs themselves. If skill, training and responsibility were spread downwards, throughout the hierarchy of work, there would be fewer issues to divide workers.

12.
Trade-union organisation

Shop stewards' committees / the membership /
full-time officers / dealing with consultants /
education and training / rights of stewards and
safety reps / collective or individual?

The employer who brings in work study and incentive
schemes is seeking major changes in the control and organisation
of the workplace. For manual workers, some of these changes may
not be immediately visible. They will occur first in the offices, as
new procedures for tighter control of costing, budgeting and production scheduling. Subsequent changes will be more obvious –
alterations in work methods, workplace layout, demarcation,
custom and practice, staffing levels and, perhaps, new technology.
Lastly, there are the changes in traditional bargaining methods,
new 'rules' for assessing a day's work, and new ways of determining pay, all based upon management's newly-acquired knowledge
of work organisation, official and unofficial.

The trade-union organisation which is totally prepared for
this purge is a rarity; usually it seems to be a case of learning as you
go and, often, learning too late. Management will buy or recruit
virtually all the expertise it requires to bamboozle trade-union
representatives with jargon, so-called logic, 'common sense' and
the rules of the game.

This chapter looks at some of the issues which will confront
trade-union organisation at the workplace. How they are dealt
with will determine their impact on the membership, their jobs
and their pay — and the way management makes its decisions.

Shop stewards' committees

A joint committee of stewards from all unions within the site
is an absolutely essential first step for workers facing the introduction of work study. A joint union approach to any employer's

proposals is the only safeguard against the workforce being split into small, self-interested groups without the solidarity and ability to mount an effective challenge to the employer in the future. A number of issues have to be investigated, debated and decided. Is work study to be allowed in the first place? Under what conditions? What guarantees are required? Even on these broad preliminary issues, it is obviously futile to respond to the employer with five or six different points of view.

Some groups or unions may object to PMTS, others may prefer shorter working time plus cash to a straightforward bonus scheme. Method changes, new technology and new equipment may disrupt traditional skills and demarcation lines. Simple changes in one section may have consequences for jobs in another. If these issues are not tackled on a joint union basis from the very beginning, management will be the only common denominator between a series of isolated and, possibly, divided groups.

The main agreement covering the general application of work study, the **work specification part one**, should apply right across the shop. It should state in detail the study methods permitted, the general nature of any bonus scheme or alternative, a firm commitment that no changes will be made without union approval, the right of access to all necessary information, facilities for union representatives and guarantees on jobs, training and pay. Once the team of consultants is actually inside the workplace, reports, studies, statistics and proposals will be flying thick and fast. Queries and grievances from members will increase. So will the number of times the stewards is asked to 'pop along' to the manager's office.

Any union representatives who have not obtained a cast iron guarantee that they will be allowed the necessary time off from their normal duties are risking complete surrender of control or a nervous breakdown – or both. Facilities for meetings and for storage of paperwork are also essential; if they are not provided in the main agreement, union representatives will be fighting a rearguard action to achieve them throughout the entire exercise. Management will spend hours with consultants discussing plans, proposals and estimates, and then expect union representatives to attend a meeting at short notice, without an opportunity to discuss the agenda and supporting papers among themselves beforehand. At best, this might be simple bad manners, at worst, a conscious strategy to extract an unprepared response.

Once established, the joint unions committee must monitor all proposals, reports and grievances arising from the work study exercise. The members of the committee may not always agree, but they will know the issues upon which they disagree and may have sufficient understanding of each other's problems to seek an acceptable solution. The committee *must* have the right to meet as often as is necessary and *must* have a proper room in which to meet.

The membership

Trade-union organisation is essentially about keeping the membership informed and involved; this means making reports to members, discussing their problems and finding out their views on all the issues. It is vital that the members understand what is being proposed and why; that they have the opportunity to ask questions collectively; and, ultimately, that they have the right to say 'no'. The only effective way of achieving democratic involvement of the membership is through **meetings** – in works time, if necessary. The time to negotiate this principle is *before* you have agreed to allow study engineers in the premises. Management will have all the meetings they require during works time and will not be too concerned at how often they have to meet union representatives, as long as they feel they are making progress.

Alongside the many gains which employers stand to make from work study, time off for union representatives is small fry. Management often need reminding that, unlike heads of department and works managers, stewards *represent* their members and an unrepresentative view expressed by a steward is worthless.

An additional aid to keeping the members involved and informed is the issue of a union **bulletin** by the stewards' committee. It need not be ambitious, nor does it have to appear regularly, but it should be clear and easy to read. Items could include management proposals, responses to widespread queries or statements on the latest rumour circulating the workplace.

It is also useful to insist that management produce plentiful copies of all new agreements so that each member can have a personal copy of those which affect his or her work. Some stewards and convenors seem to take the view that agreements are their personal property and that to circulate them reduces their authority and power in some way. Such representatives hinder the building of a conscious trade-union movement.

Full-time officers

Advice on liaising with full-time officers cannot be specific. Circumstances, rules and cases vary considerably. In some unions and industries, the full-time officer will be involved immediately, possibly under the terms of a national agreement. In others, the full-time officers may come in at a later stage. However, as a general rule, it is vital to keep the officer up to date with any discussion or proposals surrounding the introduction of work study. Apart from helping out with any union policies or guidelines, he or she may have considerable experience with work study and incentive schemes in other plants, and may be able to provide copies of agreements negotiated elsewhere. Keeping the full-time officer in the picture can help you avoid making serious mistakes, prevent problems in the long run, and satisfy the membership's desire to know 'how the union feels' about particular issues.

Most full-time officers have responsibility for hundreds of workplaces and cannot deal with any one as thoroughly as the local union representative can. This is especially true when examining information on productivity, costs, standard times and approved methods – the only views on times and methods that *really* count are those of the members actually doing the job. Regular correspondence with the full-time officer acts as a second check upon exchanges between the local representatives and management. Officers cannot be expected to assist in resolving a problem, if they know nothing of the background. Nor can they be expected to bail out the steward whose solo performances have landed the members with a long-term problem.

Unfortunately, most full-time officers will be quite unfamiliar with work study and related incentive schemes. Many, even those aware of the implications for collective bargaining, will still *support* the introduction of incentive working as a comparatively easy route to a wage increase. Any work group which has examined the issues and resolved to reject work study, may not find support from trade-union officialdom. The management ideology of linking earnings to effort has gained such wide acceptance on both sides of industry that anyone arguing against it may be dismissed as perverse or 'ultra-leftist'.

Membership understanding and support for an anti-work study position is absolutely *essential* if it is to command respect. It takes careful thought, reasoned argument and hard work for union representatives to carry a large majority of the membership in opposing what is seen as the 'common sense' position. Split meetings, with crucial votes won by the tiniest of margins, are of little use in a long campaign. Full-time officers will usually want to see clear evidence of members' opposition to work study before adding their support.

Dealing with consultants

Management consultants have changed their approach considerably since the days when they were known as 'time and motion men'. They are well aware of their poor image in the eyes of workers and that trade-union opposition can cost a consultancy its contracts. Today's practitioners advocate the importance of consultation with union representatives before doing anything (well, anything that might be detected). They usually stop short of actual 'agreement' but they are very strong on 'consultation', and will certainly advise management on the kind of agreements to go for.

Consultants often face as many problems and as much resistance from traditional management as they do from trade unionists. They will use any allies to overcome managerial opposition. Quite often, the union representatives can become an unwitting ally when the consultant starts to offer advice to both sides. It may seem odd to suggest that a steward would seek advice from a consultant hired by the employer and paid by the employer. However, in some circumstances, the consultant emerges as the only person who really knows what is going on; ordinary line managers seldom know more about work study than the workers they manage and are often just as concerned about their own jobs.

Because of this, and because they have no executive power within the enterprise, consultants can float ideas to both sides and leave them to thrash the matter out. If consultants begin to appear with increasing frequency at negotiations in the role of resident expert or, worse still, unofficial arbiter, this should not be tolerated. Despite the behaviour of individual consultants, some of whom are fairly human, agreements are made with management, not the consultant. If management cannot clearly articulate and explain their objectives, they have no right to be sitting at the negotiating table.

Trade unionists should first have a clear idea of what is *not* acceptable, worked out through the joint union committee, before they meet any consultants. This preliminary step is quite important as it sets the tone for what is to follow. It is necessary to be absolutely firm about union rights to information, time off, facilities for representatives, and meetings with members. Maintain a healthy scepticism, challenge statements and forecasts, and demand detailed explanations. Consultants may spend a lot of time to-ing and fro-ing between union representatives and management – and being nice to both – **but remember who pays their wages**.

Education and training

The right to independent, trade-union education in work study is essential. Training offered by management or consultants is in no way an acceptable substitute. It may be pedantic to make a distinction between 'training' and 'education' but, in this case, it is valid. Management may offer training in the techniques of taking time studies, rating, using the stopwatch and calculating standard times. In fact, this is simple training in the **methodology** of recording information; union representatives are taught to apply the rules as laid down by work study practitioners.

This is not only inadequate but dangerous; alternative views are not on the agenda. Time study is an exercise in gathering information and any person of average intelligence and a particular disposition can be trained to do it. It is not difficult to mix **opinions** with knowledge and information under the disguise of training. Rating, for example, is a matter of opinion but not any old opinion. The objective in rating training is to train the pupils to adopt the opinion of the teacher, as described on page 39.

If union representatives wish to take advantage of management training in work study techniques, they should at least be aware of the uses to which the recorded information will be put and of its potential effects upon collective bargaining. It is far more important and rewarding to participate in a **trade union** or

TUC course before considering management's generous offer. All TUC regions run courses in work study and incentive schemes and, in some cases, the TUC regional education officer may be able to organise a special course for representatives from one plant. It is worth contacting the local **full-time officer** or **TUC education officer** at an early stage, bearing in mind that union representatives have a legal right to time off for education and training which is relevant to their needs. (A list of TUC regional education officers is given in Appendix 2.) Representatives who fail to see any important distinction between management training and trade-union or TUC education, should ask themselves why management are prepared to bother with offering their own 'training schemes'.

Rights of stewards and safety reps

In a number of workplaces, management or consultants have suggested that selected workers should be trained to carry out method and time studies, and some trade unions support the policy of training **'work study reps'** from the shop floor or office. This is a matter for the membership to decide, as there are a number of disadvantages to consider along with the apparent advantages. Among the advantages are the potential accountability to the membership, access to information and expertise, and the degree of trust between the members and the study person. The disadvantages include the fact that, in any disagreement which stewards and members may have over a particular study, management will not be slow to point out that the study was taken by one of the members. A further disadvantage is that only those who pass through management's selection procedure and training programme will be chosen. Anyone who is cynical or sceptical about the techniques will fail – only believers can pass.

In the long run, accountability to the membership is often a myth, as members will seldom be given the right to re-call unpopular study reps. Of the eight trained work study reps in one factory I know, only one returned to his original job on the shop floor; the remainder either moved on into management or became work study engineers elsewhere.

The stewards' committee could decide to establish a **work study sub-committee** to specialise in day-to-day monitoring of events. While this is a sensible delegation of responsibility, care needs to be taken that 'delegation' does not become 'surrender'. All union representatives need a basic grounding in work study through a union-approved course so that a wide range of understanding on the issues is available to the membership, including the health and safety issues.

Safety reps and stewards need to operate in close liaison, especially where new equipment, methods and materials are introduced. Again this requires sensible procedures, delegation and reporting back to avoid division between stewards and safety reps. Stewards can avoid this type of situation by ensuring that safety reps are closely involved from the outset in examining the proposals. This procedure can also be supported by clauses to that effect in the main agreement or work specification part one.

Care needs to be taken over the wording of agreements covering the duties of stewards and safety reps under incentive conditions. While management will usually agree that the performance of these duties should not result in a loss of earnings to the representative concerned, they may often slip in apparently innocent qualifying clauses. An example which appears in many agreements is the clause which reads, 'Union representatives will be paid at average earnings for all time spent on union duties, **providing permission has been obtained**'. In the long run, a clause such as this enables management to impose a financial penalty or at least a delay, on any representative who wishes to pursue a matter which management would prefer to see left alone; this could particularly apply to safety reps' inspections. It should be remembered that for most of their functions, safety reps do not need 'permission' under the Safety Representatives and Safety Committees Regulations.

It is obviously an essential aspect of any incentive scheme that union representatives have some system of earnings protection when carrying out their duties. There are a number of methods for achieving this and the most appropriate will depend upon the type of scheme in operation. Some systems do not provide the guarantee which they appear to at first glance. **Individual incentive schemes** where each individual worker earns his or her own bonus are probably the easiest to work out. Almost all schemes require workers to book their time and output in some form or another and it should be no problem for a union representative to book time to 'union business'. All time booked in this way would normally be discounted from bonus calculations and the steward's weekly performance would be calculated over the remaining hours of the week. The hourly bonus earnings calculated over the remaining hours would then be paid for all hours worked, in effect paying a kind of average performance for time spent on union business. It may be noticed that management will gradually collect a significant amount of data on time 'lost' to union activities.

Group schemes, where the performance of a group of workers is calculated, need more careful attention. While it is still relatively simple to ensure that the steward or safety rep does not suffer financially, the system used can still inflict a financial penalty on the group. For example, take the situation where the absence of a steward or safety rep causes a machine or process to stop. If the remaining members book 'waiting time' it is highly probable that the bonus for the group will suffer and, as the union representative is also part of that same group, any guarantee of 'no loss of earnings' is meaningless. The same situation can occur where the steward's absence causes the performance of the group to drop through being one person short. Where it can be shown that union business, for whatever reason, has adversely affected earnings then some form of guaranteed earnings should be paid – the average of the past four weeks is a common formula.

Collective or individual?

Any bonus scheme can be arranged to work on a group basis and some schemes cannot work in any other way; it all depends upon the organisation of the work in question. For example, it would be nonsensical to attempt to calculate the performance of each individual worker on the same refuse collecting truck, or on a printing press staffed by six people. Where individual performances cannot be calculated or where team-work is more important than individuality, management will usually accept the need for the type of scheme where performance and pay are calculated across a natural group.

However, given the choice, most managements will plump for **individual schemes** even where the opportunity to devise a group or pool system exists. Their motives can be guessed with some accuracy. Trade unions are by no means unanimous on this issue and the arguments usually settle around money and who earns what. Those in favour of individual schemes often argue that they enable each worker to work at their own pace and determine their own bonus earnings. There is obviously some truth in this theory, which seems to be based upon the assumption that there is enough work to be shared equally amongst everybody. Individual schemes rarely have procedures to ensure that waiting time and 'difficult' jobs are shared out evenly, and this can become a major source of individual grievance, with implications for group solidarity. Furthermore, individual schemes can lead to the situation where weaker individuals can be pressurised by management into accepting revised methods or tight time standards, to the subsequent detriment of other workers who eventually have to use the revised methods and work to the tighter times. It is very much a personal view, but I see no value in organising members into a situation of collective responsibility through trade unionism, only to expose those workers to individual pressures. We do not normally allow individuals to negotiate their own basic rates or holidays so why make an exception with bonus earnings?

Group schemes have the benefit of averaging the effects of variations in performance, waiting time, unmeasured work, good days and bad days across the whole group, to produce a group performance. This encourages a group identity – any bonus issue affecting one member of the group affects the whole group. It should also ensure that weaker individuals are not pressurised by management and that any changes in methods or times must be approved by the group – it can also nullify many aspects of the 'blue-eyed wonder' syndrome.

This is not to say that there are no problems with group schemes. One specific problem needing careful thought and discussion can, if not resolved, cast the steward in the role of disciplinarian or unpaid supervisor. Across any group of workers, some individuals will produce consistently lower performances than others; by definition, some will be above the average and some below. There may be a number of reasons; 'off' days, advancing age, physique, health, attitudes to incentive working as well as what might be written off as 'bloody-mindedness'. Also, some members will always struggle unsuccessfully to grasp the intricacies of incentive working and, consequently, make mistakes in the way they book their work which can adversely affect performance calculations. Whatever the reason for the below average performances, the steward may eventually be pushed into sorting out the individuals responsible – not by management but by other members of the group. If a steward responds to such pressure, then the 'under achiever' is to be forgiven for perceiving that the role of steward and manager have somehow merged. It need not be the steward's job to react to pressure from a clique within the group; instead, the 'problem', if it is one, should be discussed by the whole group. Protecting older and slower workers through group solidarity is part of the essence of trade unionism as is individual accountability to the group for his or her actions.

A further source of division between workers, brought about by incentive schemes, can be management and trade-union attitudes to service workers (indirect workers as they are often called). It is by no means uncommon to find incentive schemes applied to direct production operatives, to the exclusion of those workers who service production or who generally keep the place clean and tidy. Quite often, indirect workers have to increase their pace of work as a direct result of the generally increased pace of production brought about by the incentive scheme. This situation is bound to encourage tensions between direct and indirect workers, especially if different unions are involved. Shortages of materials and hold-ups which cause direct workers to lose bonus opportunities are blamed on the laziness of the indirects, who in turn note that they now have two bosses – management and the production workers. The resulting hostility is turned inwards instead of being directed where it properly belongs – at management. Again, this situation can be avoided by establishing clear principles in advance through the joint union or stewards' committee.

13.
The declining bonus – a trade-union strategy

In the chapter dealing with incentives, emphasis was placed upon the minimum trade-union standards for incentive schemes. These were: that incentive schemes based upon standard times should pay a **minimum bonus** of one-third of the basic rate at standard peformance; and that bonus earnings should be stated as **percentages** of the basic rate. The first is aimed at gearing bonus payments to the likely increase in work effort, and the second at maintaining the relationship between bonus and basic, when basic rates are increased. In the long run, however, this may not be what the membership wants. Bonus earnings based upon output, effort or productivity have built in income insecurity; while an increase in pay of 33 or 40% may be highly acceptable, there is no reason why it must be paid as a **bonus**.

It is often suggested that workers on incentive schemes, including piecework, have an opportunity to control their own pace of work and, thereby, their earnings. This so-called control is extremely limited, as was mentioned earlier. The factors which really affect workers' pay are more likely to be under management's control. After all, workers can only control their pace of work where they are given **work to do**; workers have very little control where there is a lack of orders, a shortage of materials, a mechanical breakdown or a dispute in another part of the works. As most incentive schemes do not provide for average earnings under these circumstances, their effect is to cause earnings to drop. What this really means is that employers, correctly, see the bonus element of the wage packet as the element which can be *reduced* during difficulties of one kind or another. Very few trade unionists would allow the employer to reduce their basic rates, but cutting gross pay by reducing bonus earnings seems, oddly enough, to be in order. Of course, this is one of the attractions of incentives to employers – it produces an element of pay which, ultimately, they, not the workers, control.

There are cases where workers have concluded that having such a large element of pay at risk is unacceptable. Some stewards have argued that, if standard bonus is worth one-third of the basic rate, then part of this extra cash should be consolidated into the basic to reduce the element at risk through factors beyond the workers' control. There are a number of examples where, after a scheme has been in operation for a few years, the workers have consciously fought for a reduction in the proportion of pay covered by the bonus scheme, without losing the effect of the bonus roll-up when basic rates are increased.

In one particular plant, a group of process workers had been consistently averaging a performance of 105 on a straight-proportional incentive scheme, which produced a bonus of 40% of the basic rate. This meant that, as long as bonus payments were stated as a percentage of the basic rate, each £1 on the basic rate put £1.40 in their wage packets. Their objective was to reduce the bonus element to around 20% and below, without disturbing the bonus roll-up of 40%.

For example, a worker on £72.00 basic would earn a bonus of £28.80 and a gross pay of £100.80. In negotiations, the stewards got management to accept that the 40% bonus roll-up was an established fact, whilst achieving the consolidation of part of the existing bonus into the basic rate. The effect was to move the worker with a basic rate of £72.00 to a new basic rate of £85.00 while reducing the bonus from £28.80 to £15.80 (around 19% instead of 40%).

In subsequent years, the bonus roll-up of 40% was still added to basic rate increases and the amount of this to be consolidated into the basic rate was subject to negotiations. The end result was a much higher level of secure income, although to the casual observer, the scheme seemed to be completely adrift from the trade-union minimum objective of one-third of the basic rate for standard performance.

The example does not pretend that such negotiations are straightforward nor that the objective is easy to achieve, but it does indicate a sensible and supportable long-term strategy. The essential factors – the **bonus roll-up** and **consolidation** into the basic rate – are also issues to consider where employers propose the termination of a scheme or a move onto a new type of scheme. Such proposals are inevitable, as almost any incentive scheme reaches the stage where it has outlived its usefulness to the employer. Currently, many local authority schemes are being terminated because, in some cases, the rigid work specifications agreed in the early seventies no longer suit employers who have become disenchanted at having to negotiate piecemeal changes with local stewards. Local authority employers are proposing to 'freeze' bonus earnings at their current or average level. While this may be a benefit in terms of income security, it remains to be seen whether the bonus roll-up will still operate in future years.

Shorter working time

One of the side-effects of incentive working involving standard times and performance figures, is that workers often develop a greater awareness of **productivity issues** within their own workplace. The relationships between staffing, output, productivity and pay are made clearer where adequate information has been provided. An organised workforce, well briefed on these issues, is quite able to measure the effect of new methods and equipment and negotiate accordingly. It is quite often the case that union representatives who have had to come to grips with the complexities of incentive working, explain the issues to the membership, take up grievances, investigate mistakes, check bonus and output figures and negotiate over staffing, standard times and pay, have a better understanding of productivity issues in their own departments than the managers appointed to run them.

But all too often, since the mid-sixties, this understanding has been used to influence pay negotiations only. While the late seventies saw some progress towards longer holidays, the pressure to reduce the working week has never equalled the intensity of the trade unions' pursuit of the 40-hour week in the late fifties and early sixties. The last half of the seventies saw the rapid escalation of health and safety as a major negotiating issue for trade unionists, so much so that the old 'danger money' syndrome is dying out. Some may argue that health and safety and pay are totally separate bargaining objectives, yet any trade unionist who is closely involved knows that the cost of a safer workplace and the cost of higher earnings still finish up in the profit-and-loss account. Yet a conscious decision has been made in many, many cases not to trade off safety for higher pay.

What has all this got to do with incentive schemes and work study? Well, most of this book has been about the role of work study and incentives in raising output per worker. In their ceaseless efforts to reduce costs in all industries, so as to drive up the rate of profit in private industries, employers have a number of ways of increasing the productivity of human labour: investment in new technology; shift systems; flexibility; de-skilling; work study; and incentives, are some of those options. The immense potential of micro-electronics has forced trade unions to rethink traditional approaches to bargaining over change at work. Shorter working time as a negotiating counter to the introduction of new technology has rapidly become 'common sense' to most trade unionists, and there have been successes. Yet, so hide-bound in tradition have we become that work study tends to go hand-in-hand with bonus schemes. To put it another way, higher productivity through work study equals higher pay. The fact that the issues raised by new technology – jobs, control, quality of working life, pay – are also raised by work study has not resulted in any marked change in trade-union attitudes towards work study. This is not to suggest that work study, as currently practised, is potentially 'good' if used properly, but rather that it is potentially as 'bad' as new technology and deserves a similar trade-union response.

To apply this line of reasoning in a practical way, it may be helpful to think about work study-based performance figures in terms of **hours produced** instead of **bonus payments**. Take, as an example, a production worker working at an average normal pace and producing 240 units of output over a 40-hour week. Following the application of work study techniques and the establishment of a performance-based incentive scheme, that same worker's output will rise (at the very least) by one-third to 320 units per week. In conventional work study jargon, he or she has made the leap from 'normal performance' to 'standard performance'.

The customary approach to this feat is to negotiate a pay increase commensurate with the increase in performance, an extra 33% of the basic rate; the redundancy problems will not surface for another year or so. It is useful to pause for a moment to see what has actually happened. The worker used to produce 240 units over 40 hours, which is a rate of 6 units per hour. Since work study, he or she now produces 320 units, but before we get trapped in the normal performance/standard performance rigmarole, it is quite clear that at the old rate of working, the worker has actually produced more 'hours' worth of work': 320 units divided by an output rate of 6 units per hour is equal to 53.3 hours – 13.3 extra hours' worth of work, in fact. This, of course, is the source of the bonus payment because 40 hours at standard begets an extra 13.3 hours pay (33%). If the worker was able to take the extra hours produced as **paid time off** instead of taking a bonus, he or she would be able to work 26.7 hours the following week with no loss of pay.

To put it another way, he or she could work 3 weeks of 40 hours producing 320 units per week, banking 13.3 hours per week, so that the fourth week could be taken off with pay. The basis for this system is an acceptance of the approach that while higher productivity increases output per working hour it need not increase **overall output**.

In the example above, the worker's rate of output was raised from six units per hour to eight units per hour. If the original overall level of output was maintained at 240 units per week, then only 30 hours need to be worked. In Chapter 5, it was stated that the calculation of **standard minute values** for all tasks made it possible to produce performance figures for *all* workers, irrespective of the major differences in the nature of the jobs they performed. These same performance figures can still be used to **calculate time off**; all that needs to be done is to calculate performance as a percentage of 'normal', instead of standard, and apply that percentage to the basic working week to find how much paid time off has been earned. An example is shown in Figure 33.

Figure 33: *Calculating paid time off using performance figures*

Actual performance $= 100$
'Normal' $\quad\quad\quad = 75 \quad\quad 25 \times \frac{100}{75} = 33.3\%$
Difference $\quad\quad\; = 25$
Paid time off $\quad\; = 33.3\% \times 40 \text{ hours} = 13.3 \text{ hours}$

This calculation can be used in all situations and can be written out as a simple formula; Figure 34 shows the formula and some further examples:

Figure 34: *Applying the formula for calculating paid time off*

Formula: $\dfrac{Actual\ performance - normal\ performance \times working\ hours}{Normal\ performance}$

= *Paid time off due*

Example A
Actual performance = 105
Working hours = 40
Paid time off = $\dfrac{(105 - 75)}{75} \times 40 = 16$ hours

---

Example B
Actual performance = 90
Working hours = 40
Paid time off = $\dfrac{(90 - 75)}{75} \times 40 = 8$ hours

The system lends itself to the same kind of options which exist with cash bonus schemes; each worker could either reduce working hours according to the amount of paid time off banked or all the earned time off could be pooled and shared across the department or plant. The employer may require some guarantee of consistency but that would not be difficult to work out. Overall increases in weekly output would have to be met by taking on additional workers. Either way it means that the policy of **jobs-before-cash** associated with the introduction of new technology, could just as easily, perhaps more easily, be applied to the introduction of work study and incentives. The question of 'what's in it for the employer' is bound to arise. Firstly, there are the benefits of reduced costs through running the plant over four days instead of five, and the probability of reduced absenteeism with four-day working. However, the question is preoccupied with employers' desires and objectives; the bargain is supportable by any standards and it is unlikely that employers consider the needs of their employees when they arbitrarily inflict lay-offs and short-time working. Unemployment is not just a problem for trade unions and goverments to work out; employers too have a responsibility to the community.

Many commentators are suggesting that the future under capitalism will have fewer and fewer jobs to go round. What is happening is that there is less and less **waged work** to be shared out, which is not the same as **jobs**. While private ownership of production, supported by state manufacturing and services, continues to dominate the structure and shape of what we call work, trade unions will increasingly have to fight on the issue of shorter working time.

Amongst other things, the achievement of shorter working hours in waged labour will enable many men to discover the other world of work – that of the home and the community. This is not to suggest that the only reason for male neglect in this direction is the length of the normal working week, only that the opportunity to engage in wider responsibilities is increased. One final criticism is bound to emerge in the form of 'my members wouldn't stand for it'. One can only respond to that by suggesting that the members ought at least to be asked.

14.
Scientific management – Frankenstein's monster

The division of labour / control of work / the
growth of scientific management / the effect of
technology / industrial psychology / 'efficiency' or
democracy?

For the most part, this book has concentrated on the negotiating issues involved in the introduction of work study and related
incentive schemes. These are the more obvious and practical
aspects which workers and their representatives will immediately
appreciate. The word 'control' has been extensively used in
describing the benefits which employers expect to gain. Most
workers have no doubts about who is really in control of their
workplace, who makes the big decisions and who controls the
purse strings.

Employers' rigorous pursuit of **cost control**, for example, may
not seem to be a particularly threatening objective. Indeed, many
workers may see management efforts in this direction as guaran-
teeing the future viability of the organisation for which they work.
While nobody would advocate that materials, labour and time
should be intentionally wasted, the degree to which modern managements take cost control is damaging to the long-term interests
of workers as human beings.

Almost all management activities are motivated and domi-
nated by cost/benefit analysis. In any organisation there is a finite
amount of control which can be shared – for one side to gain, the
other must concede. Whether this control concerns discipline, the
way a job will be done, who does it and when, is entirely a matter
of control over current costs and, perhaps more importantly,
future costs. Management may concede cash in the wage packet,
which they can claw back by reducing the number of people
employed, but control is another matter. A considerable number
of employers spent the sixties and early seventies 'buying off' local

day-to-day controls from groups of workers. Piecework schemes, demarcations, and work methods are some examples. By the late seventies, they were seizing control without compensatory wage deals (again, British Leyland is a classic example).

In its fundamental sense, 'control' means deciding the **pace** of work, the **methods** of work, the **tools** to be used, **what** is to be produced and **when**. To exercise this degree of control, management must eliminate the element of chance or risk wherever possible. Skilled workers are an asset and a risk to any employer because the exercise of skill is the exercise of power. **De-skilling** jobs by breaking them down into separate tasks, each to be performed by different workers trained only in that task, is an exercise in cost control. It reduces labour costs through easier training and recruitment and transfers power (in the form of knowledge and control) from the worker to the employer.

A 'fair day's work for a fair day's pay' (whatever that means) is no longer enough for employers. *They* must define the degree of effort required and control the way in which that effort is applied. Work study is not only a technique which assists employers in this direction, but is part of an **ideology of work** which extends far beyond the stopwatch, standard times and incentive schemes.

In the remaining few pages, I would like to look at this ideology and the way in which it has straitjacketed our minds into accepting its effects as 'common sense'.

The division of labour

A throw-away line much used by work study lecturers and, regrettably, by some trade-union speakers, is the one about work study and the division of labour being used since before the pyramids were built. Some go further and suggest that the division of labour is perfectly natural and has been used advantageously by all civilisations. To some extent, this is undoubtedly true. The process of producing bread would have depended on farmers, blacksmiths, millers and bakers; a division of skills which is often referred to as the **social division of labour**.

The social division of labour allowed separate crafts and skills, each complementary to the others, to develop into a body of knowledge about the properties of particular materials, the design and use of tools, the laws of physics and nature. Experimentation with work methods was largely confined to improving the product and reducing, where possible, arduous physical labour. The benefits of the social division of labour were available not only to people as customers, but to those actually carrying out the work.

People relate to the world through their work, waged or unwaged, and the learning process itself is as important as the ultimate possession of creative skills.

Modern **industrial** division and sub-division of labour confers no such benefits on those carrying out detailed, repetitive tasks. It is aimed at shortening or eliminating the learning process and restricting the possession of creative skills; in the process, it demeans human labour to the point where those who profess to enjoy their work are considered oddities. Stitching a single dress seam over and over again, at the rate of one every four seconds while somebody else stitches another seam, makes neither individual a dressmaker. It enriches nobody except the employer and it is debatable whether or not, in the long run, it is 'efficient'.

Work study and the detailed sub-division of labour are not even intended to improve the quality of the goods and services produced. If product design is changed as a result of work study, it is not done to improve the product, but to save money in manufacture. The function of modern division of labour and work study is to *deprive* workers of their skills, to drive down the market price of their labour, to dictate the 'one best way' of organising work and to eliminate creative and deductive thinking.

It is not difficult to draw a fairly broad line between the social division of labour and the detailed task division cultivated by modern management. One only has to ask: what is the **purpose** of the division and who gets the **benefit**?

Control of work

The industrial revolution began the process of concentrating the new mechanical means of production in the hands of those who could afford to buy them. The establishment of the factory as a place (often the only place) where waged work was carried on, gave employers three immediate forms of control:

a) *who* worked;
b) *where* work was done; and
c) *when* it was done.

It is often forgotten that the imposition of this 'time/work discipline' was bitterly resented by many working people in the eighteenth and nineteenth centuries:

> even before the advent of power the woollen weavers disliked the hand loom factories. They resented, first, the discipline; the factory bell or hooter; the time-keeping which overrode ill-health, domestic arrangements, or the choice of more varied occupations.[1]

The following testimony before the Committee on the Woollen Trade in 1806 makes the same point about factory life:

> A tender man when he had his work at home could do it at his leisure; there [the factory] you must come at the time: the bell rings at half past five, and then again at six, then ten minutes was allowed for the door to be opened; if eleven expired, it was shut against any person either man, woman or child; there you must stand out of door or return home till eight.[2]

Luddism was more than the simple mob reaction against mechanisation that is often portrayed; it was a campaign against the impending disappearance of a way of life. The right to work and even the opportunity to work was beginning to be bought out by the owners of capital. The development of the factory system of production, bringing gangs of workers together under one roof, enabled employers to experiment with the organisation of work. Following the principles advocated by Adam Smith and others, the division of jobs into separate tasks was a technique quickly adopted by some employers as a means of cutting costs.

A very simple example shows how job division could reduce an employer's labour costs. Imagine a skilled woodworker who produces a cabinet in, say, 30 hours at a wage of four pence an hour – the labour cost is 120 pence per cabinet. If the employer wishes to treble output two more woodworkers can be taken on and labour costs would remain at 120 pence per cabinet. However, the employer notices that the skilled and intricate work occupies the woodworker for only 10 of the 30 hours, that some operations require only limited skills and others could be accomplished by a general labourer.

A semi-skilled worker is recruited at three pence per hour and a labourer at two pence per hour. The woodworker is then confined to the more complex work. Three cabinets are produced in 30 hours at a combined labour cost of 30 hours at nine pence an hour – a total cost of 270 pence, or 90 pence per cabinet. The labour cost per cabinet is cut by 25%.

The division of labour on this scale still left traditional skills and work organisation in the hands of the woodworker. The pace of work would be determined by the woodworker's judgement of the materials being used and the quality of the end product. It would not do to attempt to impose work methods and working speeds upon skills of which the employer was totally ignorant; worse still, without the woodworker, the employer would be left with machinery, semi-skilled and unskilled labour and no finished product. This is not to make a fetish of craft skills but rather to point out again that the exercise of those skills was, to some extent, the exercise of power.

The application of widening industrial knowledge and science to the labour process was initially aimed at boosting human muscle power. There was nothing unusual about this as workers had supplemented their own energies with those of animals, water and wind for some considerable time. The development of power tools did not necessarily threaten existing skills. In many cases, it added to them and introduced new ones. However, the intensified division and sub-division of jobs and the emergence of the prototype production line, had the quite different effect of **deliberately restraining workers' knowledge and movements** to the small task allotted to them. The production line quite clearly subordinates the workers to the line and to the product, which moves through and past them as they perform the only task for which they have been trained and the only task for which they have time.

The growth of scientific management

Frederick Winslow Taylor, often referred to as **'the father of scientific management'**, really brought together movements which had been developing throughout the latter part of the nineteenth century in Britain, France and in his home country, the United States. Scientific management was, and always will be, an analysis of all the factors which affect management's ability to control the enterprise. Taylor believed that effective management was synonymous with control and that the employer's ownership of the **means** of production and the **materials** of production could not alone provide sufficient control. Employers needed to control the

labour process itself in every detail. Taylor put into effect a systematic study and evaluation of human labour for the purpose of absorbing all knowledge of the labour process within management.

This was not a policy of *sharing* knowledge but of consciously *removing* it from one party (labour) and passing it to another (capital). The range of knowledge which was embodied within the individual and collective skills of workers was identified as an obstacle to managerial control. Taylor's methods, involving the study of limb movements, fatigue, tool design, machine feeds and speeds, work organisation and skills, were expensive to initiate and no immediate return could be guaranteed. In addition, they were not well received by the workers. However, by the end of the nineteenth century, the concentration of capital into large corporations had produced the kinds of organisation which could not only afford Taylor's studies, but could also benefit fully from the cost-saving methods which would result.

Just as we tend to take the factory system for granted and overlook the original working-class objections to its introduction, so the contemporary class analysis of Taylorism has been obscured by seventy years of its practical application. Trade-union reaction to Taylor's methods was so hostile that Taylorism was investigated by a special committee of the US House of Representatives. The underlying objective of Taylorism was clearly recognised by some trade unionists in the early years of the twentieth century. The following description from an editorial in the *International Molders Journal* is evidence of contemporary trade-union understanding:

> the gathering up of all this scattered craft knowledge, systematising it and concentrating it in the hands of the employer and then doling it out again in the form of minute instructions, giving to each worker only the knowledge needed for the performance of a particular relatively minute task. This process, it is evident, separates skill and knowledge even in their narrow relationship. When it is completed, the worker is no longer a craftsman in any sense, but is an animated tool of management.[3]

Taylor recognised that the factors already under management control did not guarantee that workers would actively pursue their employer's interests. In fact they often thwarted the wishes of employers by limiting output, 'soldiering' on payment-by-results schemes and generally exhibiting other forms of 'irrational' behaviour. Of course 'rational' behaviour was that which met with employers' approval; the fact that a construction worker would have a powerful incentive to slow down as a building neared completion and the sack became a real prospect was regarded as further evidence of workers' irrational and obstructive tendencies.

Taylor formulated the approach of scientific management into three basic principles which could be described as follows:

a) no task is so simple or so complex that it cannot be studied for the purpose of establishing a body of information and knowledge which can be used by management to control the speed and manner of the execution of that task;

b) the knowledge so acquired is to be used for the purpose of detailed planning and estimating, thus separating mental and manual labour. Removing the power of decision-making from the manual worker to management reduces the employer's dependence upon labour's willingness to use its thinking time solely in the employer's interests; and

c) management becomes responsible for pre-planning, pre-calculating, designing and conceiving not only the product produced but also the *manner* in which it is produced.

Harry Braverman described these three principles as: **1. the dissociation of the labour process from the skills of the workers; 2. the separation of conception from execution; and 3. the use of this monopoly over knowledge to control each step of the labour process and its mode of execution.** [4]

Taylor's programme was not conceived as some kind of subtle trick to rob workers of their skills and bargaining power; it was an entirely necessary development to a man like Taylor who identified passionately, almost religiously, with the aims and objectives of management. His opinion that workers were either misguided, lazy, truculent or simple helped turn his work into a glorious quest.

The essential factor which Taylor identified within the corporate structure was that workers and capital (in the form of management) were in **conflict**, their relationship **antagonistic**. He admitted that if he were a worker he would resist the introduction of his own methods with all his might, simply because the outcome would be harder work for little or no reward. Taylor's principles are a completely logical process where the aim is to vest control in only *one* of two antagonistic parties. The clarity with which he described his task puts to shame much of the psychological claptrap spewed forth by modern management who, bred, fed and moulded by Taylorism now find Taylor's stark, no-nonsense language embarrassing.

This is not to set up F. W. Taylor as a demi-god without whom management and industry would have avoided the revolutionary methods of the early twentieth century. It is simply that no person before, or since, has so clearly stated the fundamental reasons for the existence of management in a capitalist society.

Taylorism became the accepted 'common sense' way of organising and controlling industry and spread throughout the world. Even Lenin perceived it as one of the essential tools, along with soviets and electrification, with which to transform the Russian economy. A lesson, perhaps, to those who see the seizure of power from capitalists and its transfer to the state as *the* revolution.

The effect of technology

International capital has given a new dimension to the term 'division of labour'. The atomisation of jobs into constituent tasks and the effective segregation of those to whom the tasks are allocated is now being applied on a world-atlas scale. Raw materials produced in Africa are sent to Europe for manufacture and on to Asia for assembly, under policies and finance controlled from North America. The managerial revolution produced the new management departments of production control, scheduling, planning, budgeting, costing, design, organisation and methods. With them grew the army of clerical workers to collect, sift, analyse and organise the masses of information which management now required.

Employers also control the way science is employed in industry. There is a tendency to talk of new technology as though it fell like rain, or swept the world like the latest strain of influenza. Modern scientific-technical research is very expensive and can only be funded by the state or by giant corporations assisted by the state. It is no lucky accident that space technology has earthbound applications which are used to benefit the owners of capital yet attract little interest when, for example, Lucas Aerospace workers propose that they should be adapted for socially useful products.

The application of micro-technology to manufacturing processes would not have been possible without the earlier analysis of scientific management. Robot spot-welders, for example, could not have been built without the identification, separation and analysis of all the various tasks involved in automobile manufacture. The introduction of the production line, which effectively rooted workers to one spot, the detailed description of workers' limb movements and the simplification of the product to reduce those movements were all necessary preparations for the replacement of those workers when the fruits of carefully-directed scientific research were available.

In the original rush to apply Taylor's methods to industry, some managements became so obsessed with accurately detailing each step in every task that instruction cards were issued with all jobs, no matter how simple. The idea may seem laughable now yet the principle still exists. Workers assembling the amazingly complex electronic gadgetry used in the television and video industry do so with little formal training. The steps in building a master video console, which produces the visual effects much loved by television programme producers, have been analysed and recorded down to the last detail. The assembler's work station is equipped with its own gadgetry which provides the correct component, complete with assembly instructions, at the press of a foot pedal. Modern cash tills do not require the sales assistants to be able to count or, in some cases, to know the price of the articles they are selling. Equipment used in at least one fast-food chain has pictures of hamburgers, milk shakes and french fries on the keys instead of figures. When the appropriate buttons are pressed, the till shows the total price; the assistant keys how much money the customer has handed over and the till shows how much change, if any, is required.

Electricians who were once required to diagnose and repair faulty equipment now find that modern electronic hardware identifies its own faults. The electrician is simply required to replace the defective part; it is then passed for repair to somebody else, who has the appropriate training and who receives a higher rate of pay. This is not to say that new technology is 'bad' but simply to draw attention to the type of technology we get, its purpose and which sector of the establishment most benefits from its development.

The introduction of new technology in the printing industry has also eliminated creative and satisfying work – even among the traditionally well-organised compositors:

There is only one thing that can compensate a man for this disjuncture between the ability locked up in him and the reality of the job. That is the power to think, plan and make decisions about the processes of work. But this is not the role of the manual working class. 'We suggest improvements but they don't want to know.'

The only scope for using their grasp of the whole process – since capitalism disqualifies most of us from using it in work – is to deploy it in union activity. The immediate level of the compositor's fight is on the shopfloor, where the job has to be made tolerable, not just through better hours, shifts and earnings, but also through the re-integration, wherever this can be won, of formerly fragmented tasks. If chapels are strong enough they may be able to enforce a set-up where the men get a turn at all aspects of the job on a rota, rather than being partitioned off into battery-hen keyboard tapping, routine paste-up, or dancing attendance on the photosetter.[5]

With such techniques scientific management has reduced human labour in many industries to its most manageable form – that of a unit of energy with predetermined limb functions. Should this seem a little extreme, the following extract from an article published in the journal *Work Study* in 1981, may be illuminating:

Work itself is an energy directed toward an object or purpose to transform it into a condition in which the utility will command the buying power of the consumer. Other fields of engineering deal with the energy resulting from electrical, chemical or mechanical energy. Work study analysts or industrial engineers deal exclusively in the field of human energy.

Industrial engineers are responsible for designing effective usage (methods) and effective control (measurement) for this complex source of energy. For not only is the direct power of the human body used to create a product, but human power also controls the other sources of energy mentioned above and used by humans.[6]

Perhaps unwittingly, the authors of this piece seem to support something which Marxists would recognise – that labour is the only source of value. Even though the thrust of scientific management is aimed at reducing labour power to its basic constituent of manageable energy, and despite the continued development of labour-eliminating technology, without labour nothing can be produced.

In some ways this explains the 'time is money' adage. When labour power was purchased indirectly through the articles and services produced by human labour, a basic form of piecework prevailed. The price was a price per piece, or article produced, with the craftsman, artisan or labourer being the sole determinant of *how many* pieces were produced and *when*. Time equals money is given a special meaning by the production relationships established under capitalism. When labour power is purchased on a time basis (according to the number of hours spent at work) and harnessed to capital equipment, then the employer's dependence upon labour is paradoxically increased. This leads to greater pressure upon labour to utilise capital equipment to the maximum and, therefore, to the exploitation of labour with greater intensity.

The application of technology designed to **replace** labour brings a further intensification in the exploitation of the labour which remains. Compare the overhead costs to be met by an engineer responsible for a bank of numerically controlled, computer-operated milling machines with the costs to be covered by the output of a single, old-fashioned lathe operator.

The introduction, by employers, of new technology geared to the continuing principles of scientific management, will increase divisions between working people and the working class as a whole, unless checked. Opportunities for meaningful work will increasingly be confined to that part of the population which is male, white and between the ages of 25 and 45. Interestingly enough, Taylor also recognised that the detailed sub-division of labour would produce low-grade jobs which he felt could be passed down to immigrant labour.

This is precisely what has happened in Britain, America, West Germany, Sweden and Switzerland. What has also happened is that this 'lower grade' work, along with much of the clerical back-up for management control systems, is being carried out by women. The reduction of industrial training in many jobs to the level necessary to perform limited tasks, offers no advancement to more purposeful work. For example, the women at the video assembly plant will never become electricians nor will they learn the principles of electronics; the 'skills' they have learned are useless elsewhere.

Yet this is still only the beginning. The division of labour and subsequent de-skilling, now familiar within manual work, is being extended to the lower reaches of management. Those same clerical occupations which grew with the tide of scientific management and the growth of large corporations, now face the prospects of job division and new technology. The job of a clerk, with a wide range of duties, has been reduced to that of typist, with the invention and development of the typewriter. The typing pool may be the white-collar analogy to the production line, with the word processor, instead of robots. decimating jobs.

The pattern repeats itself: first, circumscribe the job within some kind of hierarchy; secondly, determine who should exercise and be trained in certain skills (trade unions have also been guilty in this respect); thirdly, analyse those skills and fragment the job into a series of tasks; and fourthly, develop machinery and equipment which can perform the simplified task.

Mike Cooley, the former TASS steward and member of the Lucas Aerospace Combine Committee, points out that this same process is occurring in the scientific and technical occupations:

> The welder at General Motors who takes a robotic welding device and guides its probes through the welding procedures of a car body is on the one hand building skill into the machine, and on the other hand de-skilling himself. The accumulation of years of welding experience is absorbed by the robot's self-programming systems and will never be forgotten. Similarly, mathematicians working as stressmen in an aircraft company may design a software package for the stress analysis of airframe structures and suffer the same consequences in their jobs. In each case they have given part of themselves to the machine, and in doing so have conferred life on the object of their labour – but now this life no longer belongs to them but to the owners of the object.[7]

We have all heard the management line about robots – 'they don't rest, they don't take tea breaks and they never go on strike.' However, as has been pointed out, they don't buy cars either. But doesn't the joke contain more than just an element of seriousness? What are the long-term consequences of intensifying labour productivity to the point where a vast pool of unemployment is created? We are told that there are markets opening up all over the world and that we must *fight* to *win* them. This is the language of competition and, ultimately, of war; and who will we be fighting but other industrialised countries, with jobs going to the victors and unemployment to the losers?

We were told that new technology itself would provide job opportunities in manufacturing leisure equipment incorporating the micro-processor. What was overlooked by people who subscribed to that particular point of view was that micro-electronic equipment will build micro-electronic equipment. But the 'powers that be' cannot allow mass unemployment to continue, can they? Surely something will be done and things will get better? Unfounded expressions of hope ignore the fact that capitalism is not a broad strategy, it is not a detailed master plan and it has no goal beyond its continued existence. Its basic traits are competition, individualism and aggression. At its peak, flourish the giant transnational corporations owing no allegiance to any nation, state, plant or group of people, other than a minority of shareholders. The giant corporation's strategy does not include the health, welfare and education of the people in the countries where it chooses to operate. That the pursuit of profit renders thousands unemployed is not the corporation's concern, any more than the long-term effects of its policies. Capital is capital and those who manage it can do nothing else but aim to ensure its growth and continuity.

Industrial psychology

The continued dependence upon labour has led employers to seek more sophisticated means of dealing with their 'labour problem', particularly where workers have combined in trade unions to defend and press their interests. Detailed control and sub-division of labour did not affect workers' 'irrational' behaviour, except, perhaps, to deepen hostilities. Having deprived many forms of work of any meaning or fulfilment, employers bemoaned their employees' lack of initiative and commitment.

Fortunately for employers, the behavioural scientists were ready to enter the industrial arena. Enlightened by years of studying rats, they were unleashed upon the real thing. Braverman called them the 'human maintenance crew'; their aim being to adjust the workers to their soul-destroying tasks (Marx having identified the 'problem' half a century earlier as one of the manifestations of alienation).

Not to be defeated, employers have produced the 'human relations' school, worker participation, job enrichment, job evaluation, profit sharing and countless motivation theories and techniques including one of the newer ideas – quality circles.

The purpose behind these manipulative schemes is very simple; in a capitalist society they can only have relevance if they reduce costs, particularly labour costs. Take the Volvo experiment in which teams of workers assemble complete cars, instead of working at a 'traditional' production line. The new system *may* have been preferred by the workers involved; it *may* have made work more interesting, but these are not the factors by which management will have judged the success or failure of the experiment. Unless human preference and fulfilment can be translated into cost savings by reducing absenteeism, labour turnover (and therefore training costs), strikes, and reject rates, *and* increase output, it has no value to employers. Human happiness is thus cost/benefit analysed.

The manner in which industrial society has developed has meant that our expectations have been determined solely within the confines of capitalism. In the same way, our ideas about work itself have become disconnected from all other human needs except one – money. This has not happened voluntarily, nor is it simply 'human nature' (whatever that might be); as workers we have been systematically manipulated into accepting what is handed to us. This has been one of the main purposes of the psychologist in industry. As with Taylorism, the earlier exponents are much more forthright than their modern counterparts. Hugo Münsterberg provided the following basic principles in 1913:

> We ask how we can find the men whose mental qualities make them best fitted for the work which they have to do; secondly, under what psychological conditions we can secure the greatest and most satisfactory output of work from every man; and finally, how we can produce most completely the influence on human minds which are desired in the interests of business.[8]

Adapting the individual to the task, both physically and mentally, as a branch of scientific management, is not without its critics from within. James A. C. Brown, a psychologist, rather sharply observed that,

> we cannot understand the attitudes of either management or workers unless they are seen in their historical context, and unless we realize that much that has been regarded as due to 'human nature' is, in fact, purely the product of a particular culture at a particular stage of its development. The beliefs that work is an unpleasant necessity, that the individual is basically self-interested, basically lazy, and basically competitive, that society consists of a mass of unorganised individuals, each at war with the other, that the human body is a machine to which a mind is somehow attached; that fear of starvation is the main negative incentive and money the main positive one – all these are products of a certain type of society at a certain stage in its development. They correspond to no fundamental human traits, and, even when they were most generally accepted, were never true of more than a minority of the members of industrial society.[9]

Unfortunately, having identified various common beliefs about social attitudes and human nature as the products of 'a certain type of society' (that is, capitalism), he fails to follow this through with any serious analysis of the basis of that society. Instead, James Brown suggests that moral and social re-alignment is to be found through applied reading of the New Testament. (Isn't there something in the Old Testament which gives a rich man as much chance of entering heaven as a camel attempting to pass through the eye of a needle?)

Modern methods of organising and controlling the productive processes have gained such acceptance as the 'natural' order of things, that it is difficult to conceive of alternatives.

'Efficiency' or democracy?

It has been estimated that in attempting to cultivate the right conditions for the revitalisation of capital in the UK, the Conservative government spent over ten billion pounds in benefits and lost taxes in 1981 alone. Of course, these are balance sheet statistics – pounds and pence, dollars and cents; there is no way of recording the degree of human suffering, deprivation and future blight which lie behind them. Similarly, balance sheets of the 'successful' companies exclude the costs of environmental pollution, stress, industrial disease, third world starvation and war. Imagine what would happen if US armaments manufacturers had to pay compensation for all those killed and wounded in Vietnam.

If necessary, we have to redefine **efficiency** to recognise all these factors. It is not enough to advocate workers' control over industry if we aim to organise production in the same way as Henry Ford. Nor is it enough to produce socially useful products under the scrutiny of consultants and work study engineers. It is clear that true participative democracy conflicts totally with modern concepts of efficiency, which require decision-making authority to be maintained within the grasp of a few. The effectiveness of democracy can only be judged by the extent to which it allows people a say in their own lives, not by the speed at which decisions are made.

The organisation of work (specifically waged work) must not be continually separated from the world of non-waged work and social life. The segregation of responsibilities for child care and community work and the separation of social life from working life are completely false divisions which only serve to weaken the labour movement's political position.

These are genuine political demands which cannot be satisfied solely through traditional collective bargaining. As the women's movement has consistently pointed out, they challenge fundamentally the view that equality is all about women having the right to work forty or fifty hours a week for the same pay as men. In the first place, that would not permit the time to engage in social life or democratic decision-making and, in the second place, there simply will not be that much wage-work to go round in the future. There are many indications that the trade-union movement is beginning to take these demands on board. To do so effectively, however, it will need to break free from the employer/employee straitjacket, broaden its base and drop any pretensions to being 'non-political'.

Defence of the status quo should not be seen as the maintenance of 'normality' but the active support of a particular political position. To challenge the present order one does not need a neatly packaged, all-questions-answered alternative. It is no great failing to admit, when pointing out the irresponsibility, inequality, greed and hypocrisy of the present economic system, that we do not have an instant solution to all problems. One only has to look around at the suffering, deprivation and widespread powerlessness within our own country to realise that the defenders of capitalism have solved very little except the maintenance of their own well-being.

References

1 E. P. Thompson, *The Making of the English Working Class*, Penguin, 1968, p. 337.
2 E. P. Thompson, ibid., p. 338.
3 Harry Braverman, *Labour and Monopoly Capital*, Monthly Review Press, London, 1974, p. 136.
4 Harry Braverman, ibid., pp. 112–19.
5 Cynthia Cockburn, 'The printers and their skills: a craft destroyed', *New Society*, 25 February 1981.

6 Haluk Bekiroglu and Jane Jackson, 'Work Measurement: The Quest for a Fair Day's Work', *Work Study*, August 1981.
7 Mike Cooley, Introduction to Stephen Bodington, *Science and Social Action*, Allison and Busby, London, 1978, p. 11.
8 Harry Braverman, ibid., p. 143.
9 J. A. C. Brown, *The Social Psychology of Industry*, Penguin, 1954, p. 276.

Appendix 1

A brief guide to PMT systems

Information adapted from *An Introduction to Predetermined Motion Time Systems*, London, HMSO 1976.

Note: None of the systems below include relaxation allowances and the times produced from the data should be regarded as negotiable. Reference in this appendix to 'elements' has a slightly different meaning to the word as used in the time study chapters; in PMTS the word 'elements' describes what might be more properly called 'basic motions' or 'body motions'. It should also be pointed out that sustained attempts to comprehend most PMT systems is likely to have a permanent detrimental effect upon your mental health.

Clerical work data (CWD)

Application
 Controlled by British Rail, the system is applied to routine clerical work.
Unit of time
 Milli-minute, equal to .001 minutes (one-thousandth).
Rating
 100 BSI.
Application time
 It is claimed that an experienced analyst requires six minutes to apply the data to one minute's work, which will contain around twenty elements.

Detailed work factor (DWF)

Application
> All types of manual and clerical work, particularly highly repetitive short cycle operations.

Unit of time
> Detailed time unit (TU), equal to .0001 minutes (one ten-thousandth of a minute).

Rating
> Said to be around 100 BSI.

Application time
> On intricate work an experienced analyst would require one hour to analyse one minute's work, which would contain approximately 150 elements.

Ready work factor (RWF)

Application
> A simplified version of DWF applied to all types of manual and clerical work.

Unit of time
> Ready time unit (RU), .001 minutes (one-thousandth).

Rating
> Said to be around 100 BSI.

Application time
> Around half an hour for one minute's work in which there would be approximately 100 elements. This time can be reduced considerably with computer programming assistance.

Master standard data (MSD)

Application
> All types of manual work, skilled or unskilled.

Unit of time
> Time measurement unit (TMU), .00001 hours (equal to .0006 minutes or slightly over one-thirtieth of a second).

Rating

Being based upon MTM-1, which used a US rating system, the rating is generally accepted to be 83 on the BSI 0–100 scale.

Application time

At least fifteen minutes for one minute's work containing approximately fifty elements. Simplified versions (MSD IV) require substantially less.

Master clerical data (MCD)

Application

All clerical activities including (it is claimed) work requiring creativity and judgement.

Unit of time

Same as MSD and MTM-1.

Rating

Same as MSD and MTM-1.

Application time

Ten to fifteen minutes for one minute's work in which there would be around twenty five elements. Simplified versions (MCD III) would reduce the time and the number of elements by a factor of five.

Methods-time measurement–1 (MTM-1)

Application

Manual and clerical work particularly of a highly repetitive nature.

Unit of time

Time measurement unit (TMU), .00001 hours (equal to .0006 minutes or just over one-thirtieth of a second).

Rating

Based upon a US rating system, the data is said to be equivalent to 83 on the BSI 0–100 scale.

Application time

Where method analysis is also required an experienced analyst would take three to four hours to cover one minute's work involving 200 to 300 elements.

Methods-time measurement-2 (MTM-2)

Application
> A simplified and more widely-used version of MTM-1.

Unit of time
> Same as MTM-1.

Rating
> Same as MTM-1.

Application time
> Around sixty minutes for one minute's work which would contain 100 to 150 elements.

Milli-minute data (MMD)

Application
> Developed by PA Management Consultants Ltd for production and maintenance work, particularly for jobs taking between thirty seconds and five minutes.

Unit of time
> Milli-minute, .001 minutes (one-thousandth).

Rating
> 100 BSI.

Application time
> Around fifty minutes for one minute's work involving 100 to 150 elements.

Modular arrangement of predetermined time standards (MODAPTS)

Application
> Industrial bench and machine work, also certain assembly line type clerical work. Office MODAPTS is available for normal clerical work.

Unit of time
> MOD, .129 seconds (nearly one-eighth of a second); said to be the time required to make a finger movement.

Rating
> 75 on the BSI 0–100 scale.

Application time

Around forty-five minutes for one minute's work which would include between 100 and 130 elements; less for office MODAPTS.

Simplified PMTS (SPMTS)

Application

Developed by ICI Ltd for manual short cycle work and for maintenance, plumbing and brick laying.

Unit of time

Milli-minute, .001 minutes.

Rating

100 BSI.

Application time

Around two hours for one minute's work involving approximately 240 elements.

Appendix 2

Contacts for work study courses

The addresses below are those of the TUC Regional Education Officers to whom queries should be addressed.

Northern Region
31 Mosley Street, Newcastle-upon-Tyne.

North Western Region
Baird House, 41 Merton Road, Bootle, Merseyside.

Yorkshire and Humberside Region
Blackgates House Annexe, Bradford Road, Tingley, Wakefield.

Midland Region
1150 Stratford Road, Hall Green, Birmingham.

East Midlands and East Anglia Region
7 Gregory Boulevard, Nottingham NG7 6NB.

South East Region
Education Department, Congress House, Great Russell Street, London WC1B 3LS.

South West Region
Guildhall Chambers, 26 Broad Street, Bristol BS1 2HG.

Scotland
16 Woodlands Terrace, Glasgow G3 6ED.

Wales
13 Gelliwastad Road, Pontypridd, Glamorgan.

Appendix 3

Further reading

Harry Braverman, **Labour and Monopoly Capital**, Monthly
Review Press: New York and London 1974.
This book cannot be recommended too highly. Braverman's
style is highly readable and his account of the development
of work, particularly the chapters on Taylor and scientific
management, is very clear.

Huw Beynon, **Working for Ford**, Harmondsworth: Penguin 1975.
Life on the line in workers' English.

Ilya Ehrenburg, **The Life of the Automobile**, New York: Urizen
Books and London: Pluto Press 1977.
An unusual and exciting account of the growth of manufacturing, finance capital and the consumer society told through
the development of the automobile.

Carter Goodrich, **The Frontier of Control: A Study in British Work-
shop Politics** (1920), reprinted with a new foreword and additional notes by Richard Hyman, London: Pluto Press 1975.
Workers versus management in 1920; you won't find this
piece of history being taught in schools.

International Labour Office, **An Introduction to Work Study**
3rd edition, Geneva: ILO 1979. Available from the ILO,
96 Marsham Street, London SW1.
Totally management orientated but a useful reference book
for those struggling with work measurement.

Jim Powell, **Work Study**, Arrow Books: London 1976.
Practical issues from a trade-union standpoint.

Frederick Winslow Taylor, **Scientific Management** (1911),
   reprinted Westport Conn.: Greenwood Press 1972.
   One to borrow from the library. No one has stated the aims
   of management so clearly or baldly as Taylor. Very readable, amusing in parts and, occasionally, frightening.

Index

Sue Ward
Social Security at Work

Even full-time workers may need to claim social security when something goes wrong. Illness, a strike or lockout, or just short-time working can cause a drop in income that is catastrophic. But many people do not know the benefits they are entitled to, let alone how and where to put in a claim.

Sue Ward explains the maze of social security in clear and straightforward language. *Social Security at Work* includes the 1982–83 rates and covers national insurance, supplementary benefits, sickness, trade disputes, industrial accidents and diseases, short-time working, family income supplement, housing benefit.

Sue Ward is the author of *Pensions*, another Pluto Press Workers' Handbook, of which *Labour Research* had to say: 'The job could not have been done better.'

£4.95 paperback

Maurice Frankel/Social Audit

Chemical Risk

A Workers' Guide to Chemical Hazards and Data Sheets

This book describes the information safety representatives should be given about chemicals used in the workplace – and explains how this information can be interpreted and used. It explains:

- Safety representatives' rights to information, and what they can do if information is refused.
- Why it is essential to know the chemical composition of products – and how safety representatives can deal with the problem of unidentified 'trade-name' products.
- What information safety representatives need about the hazards of chemicals and the handling of emergencies – and what problems they may face from arbitrary judgements and untested chemicals.
- The basic methods of controlling hazards, and the use and abuse of 'TLV' exposure limits.
- How data sheets should be used – and what can be done to detect and deal with unreliable data sheets.
- What information policies should be adopted by employers.
- How to use published sources of information to investigate chemical hazards.

£1.95 paperback

Jack Eaton and Colin Gill

The Trade Union Directory

A guide to all TUC Unions

The standard reference source for any information on TUC affiliated unions. It includes:

Addresses/Officers/Membership/Journals/General Background/History/ Organisation/External Relations/Current Policy

'An invaluable source of information' *Morning Star*

'Comprehensive and will fascinate anyone interested in the trade union movement' *Industrial Relations Review and Report*

Jack Eaton lectures in Industrial Relations at the University College of Wales. Colin Gill lectures in Industrial Relations at the University of Cambridge.

revised edition £7.50